MW01716760

LERNEXPRESS II

ALEXANDER MATHÄS
Virginia Polytechnic Institute and State University

DAVID CURLAND, editor
University of Oregon

KENDALL/HUNT PUBLISHING COMPANY
2460 Kerper Boulevard P.O. Box 539 Dubuque, Iowa 52004-0539

Photos courtesy of Films Incorporated.

Illustrations courtesy of Renate Spieler.

Library of Congress Catalog Card Number: 92-70217

ISBN 0-8403-7416–X

Printed in the United States of America
10 9 8 7 6 5 4 3 2 1

TABLE OF CONTENTS

Language Functions

- saying what you have done and intend to do
- describing what you are wearing
- ordering lunch
- expressing opinions
- giving reasons

Language Functions

- comparing living in the country to city life
- expressing personal preferences
- expressing reasons for personal preferences
- talking about holidays
- stating likes and dislikes

ACKNOWLEDGEMENTS

We are indebted to Renate Spieler, Austrian writer and language teacher, for her enthusiasm and creativity. Ms. Spieler contributed both supplementary exercises and a number of original drawings and Noble Goss did the word processing which made everything possible.

INTRODUCTION

LERNEXPRESS II is the second part of the new video series for beginning German from the British Broadcasting Corporation. The complete series consists of twenty 15-minute programs, distributed in North America by its co-producer, Films Incorporated, in two ten-program modules. **LERNEXPRESS** is designed to appeal to teenagers studying German in high school or college. The emphasis throughout is on the modeling of basic language functions by a lively cast of young people speaking at a normal speed against an authentic cultural background. **LERNEXPRESS II** was filmed in Bavaria and the focus is on the young people who either live there or are visiting the region. The presenter is again Sonja Zimmer as in **LERNEXPRESS I.**

This book follows exactly the order of presentation of the video scenes and is designed to work closely with them in order to facilitate the use of the programs in the classroom. There is no intention to replace the grammar text normally used but rather to supplement and reinforce it. Included are:

1. Partial transcripts of the dialogues, specifically those sections in which basic language patterns are established. The remaining sections have been omitted in the interest of encouraging students to rely heavily on the video itself for answers to exercises and for comprehension training.

2. Vocabulary needed for understanding the video scenes. In order to facilitate student comprehension, a large number of words from the video have been included, some of which may not be considered by the instructor as essential to a basic vocabulary for the beginner.

3. Exercises designed to test for comprehension or to reinforce specific and sometimes difficult points in German grammar. These exercises are of various types, some intended for individual home study and others for classroom use by either pairs (**FÜR ZWEI**) or groups (**FÜR GRUPPEN**). It should be noted that whereas the informal **du** (you) is used by the young people on video, we have employed the standard and more formal **Sie** in the exercises. The contrast in this usage should in itself be instructive to students.

4. Cultural and language notes interspersed throughout in order to clarify issues which may arise in students' minds.

5. A German-English dictionary intended to provide convenient reference for viewers of **LERNEXPRESS** but obviously limited in its scope.

LERNEXPRESS is available on either videocassette or laserdisc. For disc users whose player includes a barcode reader we have provided barcodes where scene titles are indicated. By inserting the appropriate disc and using the barcode reader, quick access to the desired scene can be obtained. Chapter numbers indicated under barcodes refer to location of scenes on disk.

It is the confident feeling of author and editor that **LERNEXPRESS** is the finest beginning film series for German ever produced. It is our hope that when used in conjunction with this text, it will make an exciting addition to the German language classroom.

David Curland, editor

Dänemark
Ostsee
Nordsee
Flensburg
Schleswig
Husum
Fehmarn
Puttgarden
Saßnitz
Rügen
Helgoland
(zu Schleswig-Holstein)
Kiel
Heide
Rendsburg
Stralsund
Schleswig-Holstein
Rostock
Greifswald
(zu Hamburg)
Lübeck
Wismar
Mecklenburg-Vorpommern
Anklam
Cuxhaven
Itzehoe
Bad Oldesloh
Ratzeburg
Güstrow
Neubrandenburg
Stade
Aurich
Wilhelmshaven
Hamburg
Lauenburg
Schwerin
Plau
Waren
Emden
Bremerhaven
Parchim
Neustrelitz
Varel
Buchholz
Leer
Bremen
Ludwigslust
Prenzlau
Oldenburg
Lüneburg
Cloppenburg
Soltau
Wittenberge
Schwedt
Verden
Uelzen
Neuruppin
Polen
Niederlande
Meppen
Niedersachsen
Salzwedel
Eberswalde-Finow
Vechta
Celle
Stendal
Strausberg
Nordhorn
Lingen
Bramsche
Nienburg
Rathenow
Berlin
Wolfsburg
Gardelegen
Bad Bentheim
Osnabrück
Hannover
Braunschweig
Brandenburg
Potsdam
Frankfurt
Gronau
Melle
Peine
Burg
Brandenburg
Hildesheim
Königslutter
Sachsen-Anhalt
Eisenhüttenstadt
Bielefeld
Salzgitter
Luckenwalde
Münster
Lemgo
Hameln
Magdeburg
Coesfeld
Alfeld
Halberstadt
Wittenberg
Lübbenau
Guben
Gütersloh
Detmold
Staßfurt
Bocholt
Wernigerode
Dessau
Cottbus
Kleve
Haltern
Hamm
Höxter
Einbeck
Finsterwalde
Nordrhein-Westfalen
Paderborn
Duderstadt
Torgau
Geldern
Bottrop
Essen
Dortmund
Warburg
Eisleben
Senftenberg
Weißwasser
Duisburg
Göttingen
Nordhausen
Halle
Leipzig
Krefeld
Arnsberg
Mönchengladbach
Düsseldorf
Hagen
Arolsen
Merseburg
Riesa
Kassel
Mühlhausen
Weißenfels
Neuss
Remscheid
Bad Berleburg
Korbach
Bautzen
Görlitz
Naumburg
Meißen
Dresden
Jülich
Köln
Leverkusen
Olpe
Gotha
Erfurt
Weimar
Zittau
Siegen
Bad Hersfeld
Sachsen
Aachen
Pirna
Eisenach
Jena
Gera
Bonn
Bad Honnef
Herborn
Marburg
Bad Salzungen
Thüringen
Chemnitz
Saalfeld
Euskirchen
Hachenburg
Gießen
Fulda
Meiningen
Zwickau
Suhl
Reichenbach
Belg.
Wetzlar
Hessen
Koblenz
Limburg
Butzbach
Bad Kissingen
Sonneberg
Plauen
Hof
Daun
Coburg
Frankfurt
Hanau
Selb
Rheinland-Pfalz
Wiesbaden
Schweinfurt
Kulmbach
Offenbach
Bingen
Bernkastel-Kues
Aschaffenburg
Bayreuth
Mainz
Darmstadt
Tschecho-slowakei
Bamberg
Lux.
Trier
Forchheim
Idar-Oberstein
Würzburg
Worms
Heppenheim
Wertheim
Erlangen
Weiden
Saarland
Ludwigshafen
Rothenburg ob der Tauber
Amberg
Mettlach
Kaiserslautern
Mannheim
Nürnberg
Saarlouis
Heidelberg
Schwandorf
Speyer
Neustadt a. d. W.
Schwäbisch Hall
Saarbrücken
Ansbach
Neumarkt
Landau
Heilbronn
Pirmasens
Regensburg
Baden-Württemberg
Karlsruhe
Treuchtlingen
Pforzheim
Backnang
Oberkochen
Rastatt
Straubing
Deggendorf
Stuttgart
Ingolstadt
Weil der Stadt
Esslingen
Donauwörth
Neuburg
Landshut
Passau
Altensteig
Heidenheim
Bayern
Eggenfelden
Frankreich
Kehl
Tübingen
Ulm
Freising
Augsburg
Blaubeuren
Fürstenfeldbruck
Lahr
Ehingen
Erding
Rottweil
Burghausen
München
Breisach
Furtwangen
Biberach
Memmingen
Starnberg
Traunstein
Freiburg
Tuttlingen
Rosenheim
Ravensburg
Singen
Kempten
Lörrach
Friedrichshafen
Konstanz
Lindau
Garmisch-Partenkirchen
Berchtesgaden
Oberstdorf
Schweiz
Österreich
© westermann

PROGRAMM 11

WINTERFERIEN

In this program, presenter Sonja Zimmer takes us on the train to **Garmisch-Partenkirchen,** a famous ski resort in the Bavarian Alps. She introduces us to some tourists of all age groups who are having fun skiing and ice skating during their vacation. We will also watch some interesting footage of the 1936 Winter Olympics.

LANGUAGE FUNCTIONS

- saying what you have done and intend to do
- describing what you are wearing
- ordering lunch
- expressing opinions
- giving reasons

CONTENTS

- clothing
- vacationing in Germany
- winter sports
- at a German restaurant
- table manners
- future and past tense
- subordinate clauses with **weil . . .**

chapter 1 to 8

Scene 1: On the Train to Garmisch

chapter 2 to 3

der Anzug,¨-e suit
Handschuh,-e glove
Pulli,-s sweater
Rock,¨-e skirt
Rolli,-s turtleneck
Schlafanzug,¨-e pajama
Schuh,-e shoe
Ski,-er or **Schi** ski
Skiurlaub ski vacation
Socken,- sock
Stiefel,- boot
Urlaub vacation

die Bluse,-n blouse
Hose,-n pants
Jacke,-n jacket
Jeans jeans
Jugendherberge,-n youth hostel
Kleidung clothing
Kulturtasche,-n vanity/makeup case
Mütze,-n cap, hat

das Bett,-en bed
Handtuch,¨-er towel
Hemd,-en skirt
Kleid,-er dress
Kleidungsstück,-e article of clothing

an/fangen (fängt an) to begin
aus/packen (packt aus) to unpack
bleiben to stay
frei free, unoccupied
ski/fahren (fährt Ski) to ski
ski/laufen (läuft Ski) to ski (synonym)
werden (wird) will (future)

Auf geht's! - Let's go!
Das war's - That's it.
erst mal - first
in den nächsten Wochen - in the next few weeks
Ist das Bett hier frei? - Is anyone sleeping in this bed?
Was werden Sie ... machen? - What will you do...? / are you going to do...?

Wie lange werden Sie ... bleiben? - How long will you stay...? / are you going to stay?
Woher kommen Sie? - Where are you from?
aus der DDR - from the GDR
Wohin fahren Sie? - Where are you going?
nach Garmisch - to Garmisch

Cultural Note

After World War II, the allied forces divided Germany into four sectors. With the beginning of the Cold War, Germany was caught in the increasing tensions between the Soviet Union and the Western allies. After negotiations regarding a common German future broke down (London Conference 1947), the Eastern and Western sectors drifted further and further apart until their separation became finalized in 1949. The two emerging German states were called **DDR (Deutsche Demokratische Republik)** and **BRD (Bundesrepublik Deutschland)**. The former German capital, Berlin, remained under the control of the four allies, although situated on Eastern territory in the Russian sphere of influence. Divided Berlin became a symbol of German separation. In 1961, the government of the **DDR** erected a wall, dividing the city in half, because more and more East Germans had gone to the West for both economic and political reasons. In spite of improved East-West relations since the 1970s, which made it easier for West Germans to travel to the **DDR**, it remained impossible for the majority of East Germans to go West until the wall opened in the fall of 1989. The **DDR** no longer exists, since the two German states were officially reunited on October 3, 1990. The new united Germany is called **Bundesrepublik Deutschland**. In this scene, Enrico from the former **DDR** takes advantage of the new opportunity to go skiing in the West.

A. What do the travellers on the train tell Sonja about their vacation plans?

1. **Woher kommt Enrico?**

   a) aus Garmisch-Partenkirchen   b) aus München   c) aus der DDR

2. **Wohin fahren Enrico, Knut und Christine?**

   a) nach München   b) in die DDR   c) nach Garmisch-Partenkirchen

3. **Wie lange wird Christine dort bleiben?**

   a) drei Tage   b) eine Woche   c) zwei Jahre

4. **Was wird Christine dort machen?**

   a) schwimmen   b) wandern   c) skifahren

Cultural Note

Germans are known as enthusiastic travelers. They take longer vacations than Americans. It is not unusual for a German employee to have a paid, five to six weeks annual vacation. Schools, instead of having three months break in the summer, have many shorter breaks throughout the year: **Sommerferien,** six weeks in the summer; **Herbstferien,** one week in the fall; **Weihnachtsferien,** two weeks at Christmas; **Faschingsferien** (Carnival), one week at the end of February; **Osterferien,** two weeks at Easter; **Pfingstferien** (Pentecost), one week at the end of May. This is why it is easy for German families to go on vacation two or three times a year.

Grammar

<u>Present Tense</u>	<u>Future Tense</u>
Ich **fahre** nach Garmisch.	Ich **werde** nach Garmisch **fahren**.

Note: Present and future are often used interchangeably.

B. **<u>FÜR ZWEI</u>**

Wohin werden Sie im Urlaub fahren? Was werden Sie dort machen? Talk to your partner about your plans for the next vacation!

Was werden Sie in den Ferien machen?

	in den Bergen	**skilaufen**
Ich werde	**in einem Restaurant**	**arbeiten**
	zu Hause	**bleiben**
	bei meinen Eltern	**wohnen**
	?	**?**

C. Write a paragraph about your plans for your next vacation. Use the future tense.

D. **Im Jahr 2050!**

1. Wie alt werden Sie sein?
2. Wo werden Sie arbeiten und wohnen?
3. Was werden Sie essen?
4. Was werden Sie in der Freizeit machen?
5. Wie wird die Umwelt (environment) aussehen?

E. **<u>Alles klar</u>?**

In der Jugendherberge in Garmisch

After Sonja arrives in the youth hostel in Garmisch, she introduces herself to her roommates and asks them politely if she can occupy a certain bed. What does she say?

____?

If you are in a restaurant and would like to know if you can sit at a certain table, you use the same sentence pattern. What do you say?

____?

Sonja fängt erst mal an auszupacken. Was hat sie mitgebracht?

1. ____________ 2. ____________ 3. ____________

4. ____________ 5. ____________ 6. ____________

Welche Kleidungsstücke tragen (wear) **Sie heute? b) im Winter c) im Sommer?**

F. **FÜR GRUPPEN**

Was ist in meinem Koffer?

You have packed your suitcase for a winter vacation. Show the others in pantomime what is in your suitcase. The others have to name the objects. Show three to five objects, then change roles.

G. **FÜR ZWEI**

Winterferien in Garmisch

Imagine you are going on a skiing vacation to Garmisch together. Plan your trip:

- When will you go?
- How will you get there?
- How long will you stay?
- Where will you stay and how much would it cost?
- What will you do there (during the day, at night)?

H. **FÜR GRUPPEN**

Pick one of the students in class and write down what she or he is wearing today. Then read your notes to the class. The student who guesses the name of the person you described then reads his/her own description.

Scene 2: On the Ski Slopes

chapter 3 to 4

der Anfang,¨-e beginning
Schnee snow
Spaß,¨-e fun

die Angst,¨-e fear
Seite,-n side

fallen, fiel, gefallen to fall down
sich erinnern to remember

ängstlich frightened, scared
auch also
dreieinhalb three-and-a-half
eigentlich actually

ein bißchen a little
leicht easy
recht quite
schwer hard
schwierig difficult
seit since, for
so ein such a
ungefähr about, approximately
ungewohnt new, unaccustomed

Angst haben to be afraid
als Kind as a child
es macht Spaß it's fun
zum ersten/zweiten/dritten Mal for the first/second/third time

Grammar

<u>Perfect Tense</u>	<u>Present Tense</u>
How long have you been skiing?	**Seit wann laufen Sie Ski?**
I have been skiing for 30 years.	**Ich laufe schon seit 30 Jahren Ski.**

To express the duration of an ongoing action or habit that began in the past, German uses the present tense.

Sonja: Woher kommen Sie?
Liesl: Aus Garmisch-Partenkirchen.
Sonja: Seit wann laufen Sie Ski?
Liesl: Seit 30 Jahren.
Sonja: Ist das schwierig?
Liesl: Wenn man als Kind anfängt, ist es leicht, aber es hat auch schwierige Seiten, das Fahren.

Sonja: Woher kommen Sie?
Frank: Ich komme aus der Nähe von Frankfurt.
Sonja: Seit wann laufen Sie Ski?
Frank: Seitdem ich dreieinhalb bin.
Sonja: Ist es schwierig, es zu lernen?
Frank: Kann ich mich nicht mehr erinnern, aber meine Schüler, die lernen es eigentlich recht schnell.

I. <u>Alles klar</u>?

1. **Wie alt ist Gabriele?**

   a) drei b) vier c) fünf

2. **Zum wievielten Mal fährt Gabriele heute Ski?**

   a) zum ersten Mal b) zum zweiten Mal c) zum dritten Mal

3. **Wie alt ist Maximilian?**

   a) fünfzehn b) vier c) fünf

4. **Zum wievielten Mal fährt Maximilian heute Ski?**

   a) zum dritten Mal b) zum zweiten Mal c) zum ersten Mal

5. **Woher kommt Jutta?**

   a) aus Garmisch b) aus Hamburg c) aus Mittenwald

6. **Seit wann läuft sie Ski?**

   a) seit fünfzehn Jahren b) seit fünfzig Jahren c) seit fünf Jahren.

J. **FÜR VIER**

Winterferien, Fortsetzung

Now you have been in Garmisch for several days. You meet two other people whom you did not know before. Find out:

- Where the people come from?
- What their names are?
- How long they have been there?
- How long they are going to stay?
- What they have done there so far and what they are going to do?
- What was fun? Was there something they did not like?
- Plan on doing something together!

Grammar Review

If you talk to a fellow student you use the **du** form. Whenever you talk to people such as your employer, your teacher, or an older stranger, you say **Sie.**

du gehst	**Sie** gehen
du kommst	**Sie** kommen

K. **<u>Und Sie</u>? Seit wann?** Get together with a partner and interview each other! (take notes)

1. Seit wann lernen Sie Deutsch?

   ____.

2. Seit wann studieren Sie?

   ____.

3. Seit wann fahren Sie Auto?

   ____.

4. Was macht Ihnen Spaß?

   ____.

5. Seit wann haben Sie ein Hobby?

   ____.

L. **FÜR ZU HAUSE**

Write a paragraph about your partner's habits using the information that you gathered in the interview.

Scene 3: Ordering Lunch

chapter 4 to 5

der **Appetit** appetite
Glühwein,-e mulled wine
Kaiserschmarren sweet Austrian pancake
Kartoffelsalat,-e potato salad
Käse,- cheese
Leberkäse,- German meat loaf
Salat,-e salad
Wein,-e wine

das **Knackwürstchen,-** small crunchy sausage
Salz salt
Weizenbier, -e German (light) beer
Wiener Schnitzel veal steak
Würstchen, - small sausage

die **Kartoffel, -n** potato
Pommes Frites (pl.) French fries
Wurst,¨-e sausage

ausgezeichnet excellent
einmalig excellent
fantastisch marvellous
garniert garnished
gemischt mixed
gerade right now
knackig crunchy
perfekt perfect
toll great
wunderbar wonderful

Leberkäse garniert

Bitte schön? - What can I do for you?
Bitte schön! - Here you are!
Grüß Gott! (southern German) = **Guten Tag!**
Guten Appetit! - Good appetite! (Said at the start of a meal) **Ich hätte gern...** - I would like...
Schmeckt das? - Does it taste good?
Wieviel hat es gekostet! - How much was it?

Waiter:	Grüß Gott, bitte schön?
Sonja:	Ich hätte gerne einen Leberkäse garniert und einen Glühwein.
Waiter:	Bitte schön. Guten Appetit.
Sonja:	Sagen Sie, was essen Sie da gerade?
Woman:	Ich glaube, das ist Kaiserschmarren.
Sonja:	Wieviel hat der gekostet?
Woman:	Das weiß ich gerade nicht. 11 Mark fünfzig.
2nd woman:	Ich esse Kartoffelsalat mit vier kleinen Knackwürstchen.
Sonja:	Und schmeckt das?
2nd woman:	Ja, sehr gut. Der Kartoffelsalat ist einmalig. Die Würstchen sind sehr knackig, weil man ja Knackwurst sagt. Es ist ganz fantastisch. Und natürlich das tolle Weizenbier ist ganz toll.

Cultural Note

Germans usually use both hands to eat, holding the fork in the left and the knife in the right hand. They hold on to their knives even after they have finished cutting the meat, because they also use the knife to push the noodles or potatoes onto their fork. It is not considered polite to keep one hand under the table.

M. **Alles klar?**

1. **Was ißt der Herr?**

   a) ein Wiener Schnitzel mit Kartoffelsalat
   b) ein Knackwürstchen mit gemischtem Salat
   c) ein Wiener Schnitzel mit Pommes Frites und gemischtem Salat

2. **Was hat der Kaiserschmarren gekostet?**

   a) DM 10,50   b) DM 11,20   c) DM 11,50

3. **Wie schmeckt der Kartoffelsalat?**

   a) knackig   b) einmalig   c) toll

> ***Cultural Note***
>
> In German restaurants the **Kellner/in** (waiter/waitress) does not normally come around often during the course of your meal. You will also have to get the attention of the person in charge when you are finished eating and would like to pay. In this case you say: **Die Rechnung** (the check), **bitte!** or if it is a small amount, **Zahlen, bitte!** The tip is usually included in the check. Because the salaries of waiters and waitresses are low, most people give a tip anyway, between 5 and 10 percent of the total.

N. **FÜR ZWEI**

Was essen Sie gern? Haben Sie ein Lieblingsgericht (favorite dish)? Go through the list and find out what your partner's favorite dishes are.

Wie	**schmeckt/schmecken Ihnen**	**Kartoffelsalat**	
	finden Sie	**Kaiserschmarren**	
		Leberkäse	
		Knackwürstchen	**?**
		Pommes Frites	
		Wiener Schnitzel	
		Gemüse	
		Fleisch	
		Wurst	
		Weizenbier	

O. Check the list after learning about your partner's preferences.

	nicht besonders	es geht	gut	ausgezeichnet
Kartoffelsalat				
Pommes Frites				
Fleisch				
Leberkäse				
Kaiserschmarren				
Wurst				
Gemüse				
Weizenbier				
Hamburger				

P. **FÜR GRUPPEN: Mittagessen in der "Loisl-Hütte"**

You have had a good workout skiing all morning. Now you are going to have lunch at the "Loisl-Hütte" where the food is good and the service is especially friendly. One of you will be the waiter, the others are guests. Start the conversation by asking for the menu, then choose a dish from the menu shown below. The waiter will ask you what you would like to eat. Make sure that you know the dish you order. If you do not know, ask. After you have finished eating, the waiter will ask you how you liked your meal. Don't forget to ask for the check before you leave.

Kellner: Grüß Gott, bitte schön?
Gast: Ich hätte gerne....
(after waiter comes back with meals)
Kellner: Bitte schön. Guten Appetit!
(after you're finished eating)
Gast: Die Rechnung, bitte!
Kellner: Das macht zusammen...

Scene 4: At the Olympic Ski Stadium

chapter 5 to 6

Cultural Note

The 1936 summer Olympics took place in Berlin. The winter Olympics took place in Garmisch. Compared with today the financial gains for the top athletes were small. Besides their medals, the only thing the German athletes received were two pounds of sugar.

On Screen

Hitler eröffnete die Olympischen Winterspiele 1936. 755 Wettkämpfer aus 28 Ländern nahmen an den Spielen teil. Eine halbe Million Zuschauer kamen zu den Wettkämpfen.

Hitler introduced the 1936 Winter Olympics in which 755 contestants from 28 countries took part. Half a million people came to watch the contests.

Scene 5: At the Ice-Skating Rink

chapter 6 to 7

der Schlittschuh,-e ice-skating shoe
Freund,-e friend

das Paar,-e pair, couple

die Größe,-n size
Leute (pl.) people
Luft air

frisch fresh
halt (coll.) you know
herum/fahren (fährt herum) to move around
manchmal sometimes
natürlich of course, sure
regelmäßig regularly
rum = herum around
schon already
sportlich athletic
treffen (trifft) to meet

ab und zu now and then
an der frischen Luft in the open air
Es geht schon. It's all right.

Skater: Ein Paar Schlittschuhe, bitte.
Clerk: Welche Größe bitte?
Skater: 40.
Clerk: 5 Mark, bitte.
Skater: So, bitte schön.
Clerk: Danke.

Sonja: Das Wetter ist echt schön zum Eislaufen. Es ist sehr voll, da es Sonntag ist.

Q. <u>Alles klar</u>?

1. **Wie alt ist Elke?**

   a) neunzig b) neunundzwanzig c) neunzehn

2. **Wie alt ist Sandra?**

   a) acht b) achtzig c) achtzehn

3. **Seit wann fährt sie Schlittschuh?**

   a) seit 5 Jahren
   b) 15 Jahren
   c) 5 Wochen

4. **Wie oft fährt Sandra Schlittschuh?**

   a) jeden Tag
   b) ab und zu
   c) immer

5. **Seit wann fährt Arnold Schlittschuh?**

   a) seit dreizehn Monaten
   b) seit drei Jahren
   c) seit drei Wochen

6. **Warum macht Sabine das Schlittschuhfahren Spaß?**

   a) weil es schwierig ist b) weil man Freunde trifft c) weil das Wetter immer schön ist.

> *Grammar*
>
> Using sentences with **weil** when responding to questions introduced by **warum**:
>
> Example: **Warum** fährst du ? - **Weil** es Spaß macht.
> **Warum** macht Sabine das Schlittschuhlaufen Spaß? - **Weil....**

R. **FÜR ZWEI**
Ask your partner why he or she does the following activities:

Beispiel: Warum essen Sie so viele Pommes Frites? Weil sie mir schmecken.

Warum....

essen Sie	(k)einen Leberkäse? so viele (keine) Pommes Frites?	
fahren Sie (nicht)	in Urlaub? Fahrrad?	
lernen Sie tragen Sie	Deutsch/Französisch/Spanisch? einen Wintermantel? eine kurze Hose?	**Weil...**
trinken Sie	so viel Weizenbier?	

Scene 6: At a Youth Hostel

chapter 7 to 8

der Ausflug,¨-e excursion
Berg,-e mountain
Hausberg,-e a name of a mountain

das Snowboard,-s

dabei sein to come along; participate
kennen/lernen (lernt kennen) to get to know
unter/nehmen (unternimmt) to do

Im nächsten Interview erzählen Elisabeth und Cornelia, was sie heute gemacht haben und was sie morgen machen werden.

Sonja: Wie alt bist du, Cornelia?
Cornelia: Ich bin 17 Jahre alt.
Sonja: Was hast du heute gemacht?
Cornelia: Ich war heute beim Skifahren am Hausberg.
Sonja: Was wirst du morgen unternehmen?
Cornelia: Morgen machen wir einen Ausflug nach München.
Sonja: Bist du gerne ohne deine Eltern im Urlaub?
Cornelia: Ja.
Sonja: Warum?
Cornelia: Man kann sehr viele junge Leute kennenlernen.

Sonja: Wie alt bist du, Elisabeth?
Elisabeth: Ich bin 16 Jahre alt.
Sonja: Was hast du heute gemacht?
Elisabeth: Ich war heut' beim Eislaufen.
Sonja: Was wirst du morgen unternehmen?
Elisabeth: Ich geh' zum Skifahren auf die Zugspitze.
Sonja: Bist du gerne ohne deine Eltern im Urlaub?
Elisabeth: Ja, man ist ungebundener (freier).

There are several options for expressing the past and the future tense.

Past ➨ skifahren - Ich war beim Skifahren = Ich war Skifahren.

Present ➨ machen - Was wirst du machen? **oder** Was machst du?

S. <u>Alles klar</u>?

1. **Was haben sie heute gemacht?**

Cornelia: *Sie war heute beim Skifahren am Hausberg.* ______

Elisabeth: ______

Christoph: ______

Marion: ______

2. **Was werden sie morgen machen?**

Cornelia: ______

Elisabeth: ______

Christoph: ______

Marion: ______

3. **Warum sind sie gern ohne ihre Eltern im Urlaub?**

Cornelia: ______

Elisabeth: ______

Christoph: ______

Marion: ______

T. **FÜR ZWEI**

1. Was haben Sie **heute** gemacht? Was werden Sie **morgen** machen?

______

2. Was haben Sie im **letzten Sommer** gemacht? Was werden Sie **nächsten Sommer** unternehmen?

______

3. Was haben Sie **vor 5 Jahren** gemacht? Was werden Sie **in 5 Jahren** machen?

______

4. Welche Probleme hatte die Generation Ihrer Eltern? Welche Probleme wird die Generation Ihrer Kinder haben?

______

U. **Write a paragraph on each of the topics above.**

V. **FÜR ZU HAUSE**

If you had to describe yourself by naming the things that are fun for you and those that are not, what would you say? Think about different aspects of life, such as family, school, friends, hobbies, etc. Name five things and give the reason why each thing is or is not fun for you. Use "**Spaß machen**" and follow the pattern:...**macht mir Spaß, weil.../ ...macht mir keinen Spaß, weil ...**

PROGRAMM 12

IN DEN BERGEN

In this episode we join Sonja on her winter vacation in the Bavarian resort town Garmisch-Partenkirchen. After Sonja introduces some local high school students, we get a chance to meet Christine's family. We learn about the advantages of living in the mountains. Finally, Anton, an apprentice violin maker, shows us Mittenwald, another well-known resort town in the Bavarian Alps close to the Austrian border. There, we can participate in the celebration of an old Catholic tradition: **Fasching** (carnival/Mardi gras).

LANGUAGE FUNCTIONS

- comparing living in the country to city life
- expressing personal preferences
- expressing reasons for personal preferences
- talking about holidays
- stating likes and dislikes

CONTENTS

- family and hobbies
- talking about the environment
- **Fasching** and regional traditions
- subordinate clauses with **weil**
- difference between **weil** and **wegen**
- contrary to fact statements

chapter 8 to 14

Scene 1: Talking to Students in Garmisch

Auf welche Schule gehst du? Which school do you attend?
18 km enfernt von Garmisch. 18 kilometers away from Garmisch.

Sonja: I've been in Garmisch for a week now, and I've seen and done lots of things. Ich war Schlittschuh laufen, ich bin Ski gefahren, und ich habe viele nette Leute im Ort und in der Jugendherberge kennengelernt. This week I'm going to meet some of the locals.

Sonja: Wie heißt du?
Boris: Boris Zwettkopf.
Sonja: Wie alt bist du?
Boris: 17 Jahre.
Sonja: Auf welche Schule gehst du?
Boris: Auf das Werdenfels-Gymnasium.
Sonja: Wo wohnst du?
Boris: In Garmisch-Partenkirchen.

A. <u>Alles klar?</u>

	Steffi	**Eva**	**Christine**
1. Auf welche Schule gehen sie?			
2. Wie alt sind sie?			
3. Wo wohnen sie?			

B. **FÜR ZWEI**

Haben Sie Geschwister? Sprechen Sie mit Ihrem/r Partner/in über seine/ihre Familie.

Fragen Sie,

1. **wie viele** Geschwister/Onkel/Tanten/Kusins/Kusinen er/sie **hat**.
2. **wie alt** die Geschwister/Onkel/Tanten/Kusins/Kusinen **sind**.
3. **ob** die Geschwister bei den Eltern **wohnen**.
4. **ob** er/sie die Geschwister/Onkel/Tanten **oft besucht**.

Scene 2: We Meet Christine's Family

der Kaffee coffee
Krims-Krams stuff
Mensch,-en human being
Schlitten,- sleigh
Schlittenhund,-e Husky (dog)
Smog smog
Stadtmensch,-en city person
Wagen,- cart, wagon

die Autolackiererei,-en auto paint shop
Bank,-en bank
Freizeit free time
Hektik stress, nervousness
Landschaft,-en landscape, countryside
Luft air
Natur nature
Umwelt environment
Verschmutzung pollution
Zeit time

das Computerspiel,-e computer game
Gymnasium, pl. **Gymnasien** high school, prep school
Poster,- poster
Spiel,-e game
Stereogerät,-e stereo

genießen to enjoy
sich beschäftigen mit to be occupied with, to engage in
spannen vor to put in front of a wagon
trainieren to train
verbringen mit to spend with

am Wochenende on the weekend
einmal am Tag once a day
es geht nicht so hektisch zu life isn't so stressful
freundlich friendly
gemeinsam together
genug enough
hauptsächlich mainly
hektisch stressful, hectic
überhaupt kein not at all
Was gefällt dir an ihnen? What do you like about them?
wegen (+ genitive) because of

C. **Alles klar?**

Christine: Das ist unser Haus. Das ist meine ____________________ Elfriede. Sie arbeitet in einer Bank. Das ist mein Vater ____________________ . Er hat eine Autolackiererei. Mein Bruder Franz is ____________________ Jahre alt, und sein größtes ____________________ sind in Computerspiele. Das ist mein ____________________ , das ist mein ____________________ .
Meine ____________________ und Krims-Krams.
Am Wochenende trinken wir gemeinsam ____________________ .
In meiner ____________________ beschäftige ich mich gerne mit ____________________ Schlittenhunden. Wir haben
Hunde. Einmal am Tag trainieren wir ____________________ . Mein Vater spannt sie vor den ____________________ . Dann geht's los.

> *On Screen*
>
> **Dies sind Alaska Huskies. Sie können eine Geschwindigkeit bis zu 50 km/h erreichen und Strecken bis zu 20 km zurücklegen.**
> These are Alaskan Huskies. They can reach a top speed of 50 kilometers an hour and cover a distance of 20 kilometers.

Sonja: Du verbringst sehr viel Zeit mit den Schlittenhunden. Was gefällt dir an ihnen?

Christine: Sie sind sehr freundliche Hunde, und sie sind sehr aktiv, und es gefällt mir sehr gut.

> *On Screen*
>
> **Schlittenhunde werden einmal am Tag mit Trockenfutter und Fleisch gefüttert.**
> Huskies are fed dry food and meat once a day.

Sonja: Lebst du gern hier?

Christine: Ja, hier ist genug Platz für unsere Schlittenhunde, und die Landschaft ist sehr schön.

Sonja: Lebst du lieber auf dem Land oder in der Stadt?

Christine: Ich wohne lieber auf dem Land, weil ich überhaupt kein Stadtmensch bin.

Grammar Review

Primary Endings (Ein-words)

	der	die	das	die
1. Nominative. **Das ist/sind...**	mein Vater	meine Mutter	unser Haus	meine Poster
2. Accusative. **Ich habe...**	einen Hund	eine Autolackiererei	ein Stereogerät	keine Hobbies
3. Dative. **mit/bei/in...**	seinem Hund	ihrer Freizeit	deinem Zimmer	unseren Hunden
4. Genitive. **wegen...**	eures Hundes	seiner Schwester	ihres Posters	ihrer Hunde

D. Alles klar?

1. Was macht Christines Familie am Wochenende?

___

2. Womit beschäftigt Christine sich in ihrer Freizeit?

___

3. Wie oft trainieren sie die Schlittenhunde?

___

4. Was gefällt Christine an den Hunden?

___

E. **FÜR ZWEI**

Sprechen Sie mit Ihrem/r Partner/in über Ihre Familie. (Based on your discussion fill out the following form.)

	Name	Alter	Hobby	Beruf	Wohnort (Stadt)
Ihr/e Partner/in					
seine/ihre Mutter					
sein/ihr Vater					
Schwester					
Bruder					
Tante					
Onkel					
Freundin					
Freund					

F. **<u>Und Sie</u>? Haben Sie auch Hunde? Womit beschäftigen Sie sich in Ihrer Freizeit?** Write a paragraph of eight to ten sentences, telling about yourself and your family.

Scene 3: Living in Town vs. Living in the Country

chapter 11 to 12

Sonja: Lebst du gern hier?
Magnus: Ja, hauptsächlich wegen der schönen Luft und wegen der Berge.
Sonja: Lebst du lieber in den Bergen oder in der Stadt?
Boris: Ja, lieber in den Bergen, weil, ja—das Wetter ist meist schöner, und es geht nicht alles so hektisch zu wie in einer großen Stadt.
Alexander: Ich lebe lieber in den Bergen, weil man hier die Natur genießen kann.

G. **Alles klar?**

1. Warum lebt Magnus lieber auf dem Land?

   a) wegen der Schlittenhunde und wegen der Berge   b) wegen des Wetters   c) wegen der schönen Luft

2. Boris lebt lieber auf dem Land, weil

   a) er kein Stadtmensch ist   b) es weniger Hektik gibt   c) das Wetter immer gut ist

3. Alexander lebt lieber auf dem Land, weil

   a) der Winter länger ist   b) er die Natur genießt   c) es hier mehr Kinos gibt

H. **Weil oder wegen?** Fill in the correct form!

1. Niklas wohnt gern auf dem Land, ____________________ die Umweltverschmutzung nicht so groß ist.
2. Eva wohnt gern auf dem Land ____________________ der schönen Natur.
3. Magnus wohnt gern auf dem Land ____________________ der schönen Luft und der Berge.
4. Christine wohnt gerne auf dem Land, ____________________ es genug Platz für ihre Hunde gibt.
5. Wir wohnen nicht gern in der Stadt ____________________ der Umweltverschmutzung.

I. Complete the following sentences after watching the video for a second time.

1. Steffi lebt lieber in den Bergen, weil ____

   Hektik ____________________.

2. Niklas lebt lieber auf dem Land, weil __________________ die Umweltverschmutzung

   ____________________________ .

3. Eva wohnt lieber auf dem Land, weil __________________________ die Natur

   ____.

J. **FÜR GRUPPEN**

Vergleichen Sie das Leben in der Stadt mit dem Leben auf dem Land! Machen Sie eine Liste!

	auf dem Land	**in der Stadt**
1.	______________________	______________________
2.	______________________	______________________
3.	______________________	______________________
4.	______________________	______________________
5.	______________________	______________________
6.	______________________	______________________

K. **FÜR ZWEI ODER GRUPPEN: Stadtmensch/Landmensch**

Discuss the characteristics of city life and country life with your partners. What does each of them like/not like to do? Find out who your partner(s) is/are and what they like about the city/country.

L. **<u>Und Sie</u>?**

Wohnen Sie lieber in der Stadt oder auf dem Land? Give at least three reasons for living in the country as opposed to living in the city.

1. Ich lebe gern auf dem Land, weil ______________________

____

____

____

2. Ich lebe gern in der Stadt, weil ______________________

____

____

____

M. FÜR GRUPPEN

Viele Menschen wohnen lieber auf dem Land, weil es nicht so viele Umweltprobleme (problems with the environment) **gibt. Bilden Sie Gruppen und diskutieren Sie, welche Umweltprobleme Sie für gefährlich halten und was man dagegen tun kann.**

Ich finde...

die **Luftverschmutzung** air pollution		
die **Wasserverschmutzung** water pollution		
den **Autoverkehr** traffic		**schlimm** bad
das **Waldsterben** dying of the forest	**besonders**	**ernst** serious
die **Überbevölkerung** overpopulation		**gefährlich**
die **Energieverschwendung** waste of energy		**wichtig**
die **Atomkraft** nuclear power		**hoffnungslos**
die **Lärmbelästigung** noise		
?		?

Was kann man gegen diese Probleme tun?

Man kann
- Energie sparen/verschwenden
- mit dem Fahrrad zur Uni fahren
- Bürgerinitiativen organisieren
- demonstrieren
- für... Geld ausgeben
- Briefe an Politiker schreiben
- gegen... kämpfen (fight)

Scene 4: Recreation in the Mountains

chapter 12 to 13

das Kajak,-s kayak

bergsteigen mountain climbing
Fallschirm springen parachuting
klettern rock climbing
rodeln to sled

Eisstock schießen curling
Gleitschirm fliegen hang gliding
rad/fahren (fährt Rad) to bike
wandern to hike

N. **FÜR ZWEI. Welche Sportart gefällt Ihnen?**

Bergsteigen Rodeln Wandern Radfahren Klettern Tennis Fußball Volleyball Skifahren	**gefällt mir (nicht), weil es**	(keinen) Spaß (un)gesund gefährlich langweilig anstrengend (tiring) teuer	**macht.** **ist.**

Sonja: The countryside couldn't be more different from Hamburg. I asked some of the young people what there is to do here — in summer and in winter.

Sonja: Was kann man hier im Winter machen?
Elke: Ski fahren, Schlittschuh laufen, Eisstock schießen, Curling, rodeln, sehr Vieles, Verschiedenes.
Sonja: Und im Sommer?
Elke: Im Sommer, schwimmen, bergsteigen, wandern, klettern, Kajak fahren.

Sonja: Was kann man hier im Winter machen?
Rina: Ski fahren, rodeln, Schlittschuh laufen, und ja...

Magnus: Man kann Ski fahren, Schlittschuh fahren, schöne Winterwanderungen unternehmen.
Sonja: Und im Sommer?

Magnus: Im Sommer kann man berggehen oder bergwandern, man kann fallschirmspringen oder paragleiten.

O. **Was kann man in den Bergen machen?** Make a list of activities.

a) Im Winter:

1. ____________ 2. ____________ 3. ____________

4. ____________ 5. ____________ 6. ____________

b) Im Sommer:

1. ____________ 2. ____________ 3. ____________

4. ____________ 5. ____________ 6. ____________

Scene 5: Interview with an Apprentice Violin Maker in Mittenwald

der **Clown,-s** clown
Fasching carnival, Mardi gras
Faschingsball,¨-e Mardi gras dance, party
Gasthof,¨-e restaurant, inn
Geigenbau violin making
Maibaum,¨-e maypole (custom of decorating a wooden pole that resembles a tree with symbols on "branches"; people celebrate the spring by dancing around the maypole)
Obermarkt part of town
Punker,- punk
Schellenrührer man in a carnival pageant wearing a traditional costume
Teufel,- devil

die **Landschaft,-en** landscape, scenery
Geigenbauschule,-n school for violin making
Gruppe,-n group
Hauptstraße,-n main street
Hexe,-n witch
Holzmaske,-n wooden mask
Kirche,-n church
Laune,-n mood
Wirtschaft,-en tavern, bar

das **Fleckerlgewand,¨-er** traditional carnival costume
Kostüm,-e costume
Treiben action

feiern to celebrate
hinaus/treiben (treibt hinaus) to expel, to drive out
schnitzen to carve
sich (zuhause) fühlen to feel (at home)
sich verkleiden to dress up
ziehen here: to move, to go

bemalt painted in color
farbenfroh colorful
verkleidet dressed up
vieles weiter many other things
voll mit full of

Sonja:	Today I've come to Mittenwald. Mittenwald is a small market town which comes to life at carnival time. It's also famous for the violins they make here.

Sonja:	Wie heißt du?
Anton:	Anton.
Sonja:	Und wie alt bist du?
Anton:	20.
Sonja:	Wo wohnst du?
Anton:	Ich wohne in Mittenwald.
Sonja:	Auf was für eine Schule gehst du?
Anton:	Ich gehe auf die Geigenbauschule.
Sonja:	Lebst du gern in Mittenwald?
Anton:	Ja, ich lebe gern hier in Mittenwald.
Sonja:	Und warum?
Anton:	Die Landschaft ist schön, und ich fühle mich hier zuhause.

On Screen

Die Tradition des Geigenbaus besteht in Mittenwald seit dem 17. Jahrhundert. Die Geigenbauschule hat mehr als 50 Schüler—sie kommen aus der ganzen Welt hierher. Die Lehrzeit dauert 3 1/2 Jahre.

The tradition of violin making has existed in Mittenwald since the 17th century. The school for violin making has over 50 students who come here from all over the world. The apprenticeship lasts three and a half years.

Sonja:	Anton zeigt mir Mittenwald. Wir fangen in der Hauptstraße an.
Anton:	Schau mal! Das ist die Kirche. In Mittenwald sind die Häuser oft sehr schön bemalt. Wenn die Sonne scheint, kann man vor den Cafés sitzen. Das ist unser Maibaum. Auf den Bergen um Mittenwald liegt etwas Schnee.
Sonja:	Viele Kinder sind verkleidet, weil die Faschingszeit angefangen hat.

P. **Alles klar?**

Watch the video and choose the correct answer.

1. **Fasching ist**
   a) im Sommer b) im Herbst c) im Winter

2. **Anton geht auf**
   a) die Sankt Irmengardschule b) die Geigenbauschule
   c) das Werdenfelsgymnasium

3. **Anton wohnt gern in Mittenwald, weil er**
   a) gern vor den Cafés sitzt b) sich gern verkleidet c) sich dort zuhause fühlt

4. **Anton wird später**
   a) Schellenrührer b) Geigenbauer c) Clown

5. **Die Häuser in Mittenwald sind**
   a) schön bemalt b) sehr hoch c) aus Holz

6. **Viele Touristen kommen nach Mittenwald wegen**
   a) des Faschings b) der Häuser c) der Berge

7. **Viele Kinder sind verkleidet wegen**
   a) der Touristen b) des Faschings c) des schönen Wetters

8. **Wenn die Sonne scheint, kann man**
   a) in die Kirche gehen b) sich verkleiden c) vor den Cafés sitzen.

Q. **Beantworten Sie folgende Fragen. Schreiben Sie vollständige** (complete) **Sätze.**

1. Wo liegt Mittenwald?

   ____

2. Was macht Anton in Mittenwald?

   ____

3. Warum gefällt Anton das Leben in Mittenwald?

   ____

4. Warum kommen viele Touristen nach Mittenwald?

   ____

R. **FÜR ZWEI ODER GRUPPEN: Meine Heimatstadt**

Imagine somebody is making a film about your hometown and you are the host. Which places would you want to show? What would you say about them?

- What kind of a town is it?
- What can you do there?
- Is there anything special about it?
- Are there any local customs?
- Do you like to live there? Why? Why not?

Discuss this in your group and write a descriptive paragraph together.

Cultural Note

Fasching is an important event only in those areas where the majority of the population is Catholic. It is a very old custom, dating back to pagan times, and it is believed to expel the evil spirits of winter. The carnival season officially starts in November and reaches its peak in February, six weeks before Easter. It ends on **Aschermittwoch**, Ash Wednesday, with the beginning of Lent, a six-week long period of fasting. Each town has its own traditional costume. In Mittenwald it is a wooden mask, **Holzmaske**, and the **Fleckerlgewand**, a costume made of many different pieces of fabric. Besides the traditional costumes, people dress up and do as they please. **An Fasching ist alles erlaubt!** Everything is permitted during carnival!

Scene 6: Interviews at Fasching Parade

Sonja: Warum bist du so verkleidet?
Child 1: Weil Fasching ist.
Sonja: Warum bist du so verkleidet?
Child 2: Weil Fasching ist.
Sonja: Warum bist do so verkleidet?
Child 3: Weil es Spaß macht, und weil es Fasching ist.

Sonja: Im Fasching sind alle verkleidet. Die Männer tragen Holzmasken. Das sind die Schellenrührer. Was passiert hier im Fasching?
Anton: Im Fasching ist hier viel los. Die Leute hier setzen sich Holzmasken auf und verkleiden sich.
Sonja: Und was machst du im Fasching?
Anton: Ich verkleide mich auch und ziehe dann mit einer Gruppe von Wirtschaft zu Wirtschaft.

Sonja: Die Kostüme sind farbenfroh. Die Holzmasken werden geschnitzt und danach bemalt. In der Faschingszeit sind die Straßen voll mit Leuten. Jeder hat gute Laune. Das ist Anton in seinem Kostüm. Die Mittenwalder treiben den Winter hinaus.

Sonja: Woher kommst du?
Adult 2: Aus Mittenwald.
Sonja: Und warum bist du verkleidet?
Adult 2: Weil Fasching ist.

Sonja: Wie feierst du Fasching?
Woman: Ich gehe auf Faschingsbälle.

S. <u>Alles klar</u>?

1. Wann feiern die Mittenwalder Fasching?
2. Was machen die Mittenwalder an Fasching?
3. Warum feiern die Mittenwalder Fasching?
4. Und Sie? Wann verkleiden Sie sich?

Grammar

Würden is the German equivalent of the word <u>would</u>. It is a form of the verb **werden** and is used to express a contrary-to-fact statement.

Example: Ich **würde** mich an Fasching **verkleiden...**
I would dress up on Mardi Gras...

implying that I am not (e.g., because I am not living in Germany)

or: Das **würde** ich nie **tun**.
I would never do that.

As with the modal verbs and the future tense, the infinitive goes at the end of the sentence (in a main clause).

<u>Remember</u>: **würde + sein = wäre** would be
Wenn ich du wäre... If I were you...
würde + haben = hätte would have
Wenn ich viel Geld hätte... If I had a lot of money...

T. **FÜR ZWEI**

Probleme, Probleme!
Get together with a partner and advise her/him what to do.

Beispiel: schlechte Noten? — Ich würde mehr lernen.

schlechte Noten	**laute Nachbarn**
schwierige Prüfungen	**zu wenig Freizeit**
zu viele Hausaufgaben	**zuviel Geld**
unfreundliche Professoren	**zu viele Touristen**
hohe Miete	**Probleme mit anderen Studenten**
zu wenig Geld	**schlechtes Essen in der Mensa**
zu viel Streß	**uninteressantes Studium**
keine Parkplätze	**keine Hobbies**

U. <u>Und Sie</u>? **Was würden Sie machen, wenn Sie an Fasching in Mittenwald wären? Würden Sie zu Hause bleiben? Würden Sie sich verkleiden? Vergessen Sie nicht: An Fasching ist alles erlaubt!** Write a short paragraph on how you could have a marvellous time at **Fasching.** Begin each sentence with **Ich würde...** (I would..).

V. **FÜR EINE/N ODER ZWEI**

Es ist Fasching, und Sie machen Ferien in Mittenwald. Schreiben Sie eine Postkarte nach Hause!

W. **Außer Fasching gibt es noch andere deutsche Feste und Feiertage.** Match each of the following holidays with the correct date.

1. Tag der Arbeit	________	24. Dezember
2. Ostern	________	3. Oktober
3. Nikolaustag	________	1. Mai
4. Heiliger Abend	________	im März oder April
5. Nationalfeiertag	________	31. Dezember
6. Silvester	________	6. Dezember

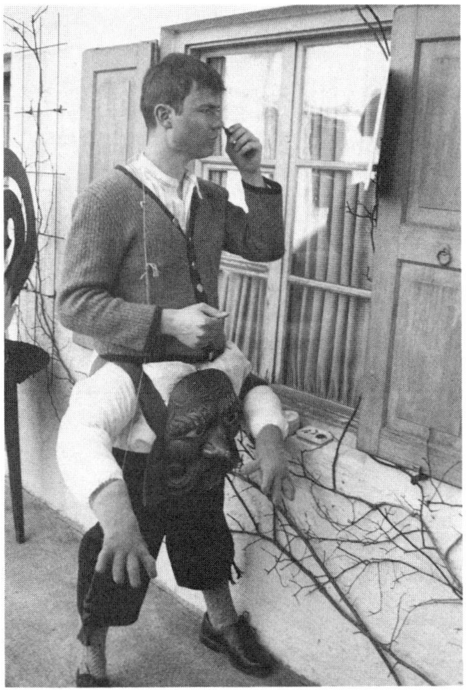

PROGRAMM 13

MÜNCHEN STELLT SICH VOR

This time Sonja shows us Germany's **"heimliche Hauptstadt"** (secret capital), **München.** First we see two video clips informing us about some of the sightseeing attractions and hotels of the city. Several professionals tell us the reason for their visit to the Bavarian capital. We learn that Munich not only has a lot to offer to tourists but also to business people. Sonja takes us to an international fashion show and then we have a chance to go to a street festival.

LANGUAGE FUNCTIONS

- asking for information at a travel agency
- talking about city life and entertainment
- expressing satisfaction/dissatisfaction
- more on stating preferences
- expressing ease/difficulty

CONTENTS

- hotels and accommodations
- sightseeing in Munich
- German cities and states
- tourism in German cities
- using a phone
- speaking a foreign language
- dependent clauses
- infinitive with **zu**
- perfect tense

chapter 1 to 7

Scene 1: What There Is to See in Munich

chapter 2 to 3

der **Eindruck,¨-e** impression
Englische Garten large park in Munich
Stadtteil,-e part of town, precinct
Video(film) videotape
Videoclip,-s video clip
Viktualienmarkt large produce market

Stadtwappen von München

die **City** city center
Folge,-n episode
Geschäftsreise,-n business trip
Hauptstadt,¨-e capital
Menge,-n crowd; here: a lot
Messe,-n trade fair
Reise,-n trip
Sehenswürdigkeit,-en tourist attraction

das **Museum,** pl. **die Museen** museum
Olympiastadion Olympic stadium
Vergnügen (sing.) pleasure

erleben to experience
etwas an/sehen (sieht an) to look at or watch something
sich vor/stellen (stellt sich vor) to introduce (oneself)
vermitteln to transmit; here: to give

bayrisch Bavarian
danach after that
erst only
geschäftlich on business
hauptsächlich mainly, for the most part
(je)doch however, yet
nahezu almost
natürlich naturally
toll great
unheimlich eery, uncanny
wahrscheinlich probably

als Tourist/en as a tourist/as tourists
einen Eindruck vermitteln to give an impression
Es geht um ... the topic is ... we are dealing/concerned with ...
um euch einen Eindruck zu vermitteln in order to give you an impression
unheimlich viel Spaß a lot of fun
zum Vergnügen for pleasure

Cultural Note

München is the third largest city in Germany with a population of 1.3 million. The largest is Berlin, 3.5 million, and the second largest is Hamburg, 2.1 million. Munich is also the capital of Bavaria. Located on the river Isar, it has many tourist attractions, such as:

Marienplatz - a large public square in the city center, in front of city hall;
Deutsches Museum - Germany's largest museum of culture, history, and science;
Olympiastadion - where the main events of the 1972 summer Olympics took place;
Schwabing - a former artists' colony with lots of bars and restaurants, comparable to New York's Greenwich Village;
Englischer Garten - a large beautiful park in the city;
Viktualienmarkt - a large permanent produce market;
Hofbräuhaus - perhaps the world's most famous beer hall;
Oktoberfest - a huge pleasure fair which draws five million visitors to the "blue-and-white" metropolis;
Dachau - a town close to Munich, the site of a former World War II concentration camp, which has been converted into a public monument.

Sonja: Hallo! Hier bin ich wieder. Ich hatte eine tolle Zeit in den Bergen, und nun will ich mir die bayrische Hauptstadt München anschauen.

In dieser Folge geht es um die Stadt. Natürlich gibt es eine Menge Touristen in München, doch viele Leute sind auch geschäftlich hier. Nun erst einmal zwei Videoclips, um euch einen Eindruck zu vermitteln—über die Hotels und natürlich die Sehenswürdigkeiten.

Sonja: Könnt ihr euch bitte mal vorstellen?

Florian: Ich bin der Florian, bin 17 Jahre alt und komme aus München.
Marco: Und ich bin der Marco, bin 16 Jahre alt, und es macht unheimlich viel Spaß, für euch diesen Video zu machen.
Sonja: Woher kommen Sie?
Woman: Wir kommen aus Hamburg.
Sonja: Sind Sie hier auf Geschäftsreise oder als Tourist?
Woman: Wir sind als Touristen hier.
Sonja: Was haben Sie schon von München gesehen?
Woman: Ach, wir haben die City gesehen—wir haben schon sehr viel erlebt heute morgen.

Sonja: Woher kommen Sie?
Man: Aus Freiburg.
Sonja: Was haben Sie schon von München gesehen?
Man: Den Marienplatz.
Sonja: Was machen Sie morgen?
Man: Das Deutsche Museum.

Sonja: Was haben Sie schon von München gesehen?
Teenage Girl: Also, wir waren gestern im Olympiastadion und danach haben wir etwas vom Stadtteil Schwabing angesehen.
Sonja: Was machen Sie morgen?
Teenage Girl: Morgen fahren wir wahrscheinlich nach Dachau.
Man: Ich komme aus Alabama, USA, im Süden.
Sonja: Was haben Sie schon von München gesehen?
Man: Nicht viel, wir sind heute erst hier angekommen.

Sonja: Sind Sie hier geschäftlich oder nur zum Vergnügen?
2nd Girl: Ich bin zum Vergnügen hier, als Tourist.
Sonja: Was haben Sie schon von München gesehen?
2nd Girl: Den Englischen Garten und den Marienplatz.
Sonja: Was werden Sie morgen machen?

On Screen

München hat 1,3 Millionen Einwohner. München ist eines der bedeutendsten Wirtschaftszentren Europas.
Munich has a population of 1.3 million. Munich is one of Europe's most important economic centers.

2nd Girl: Morgen will ich auf den Viktualienmarkt.
Sonja: Sind Sie hier geschäftlich?
Man: Ja, ich bin geschäftlich hier.
Sonja: Was haben Sie schon von München gesehen?
Man: 'Ne ganze Menge, aber hauptsächlich die Biergärten, weil die interessant sind.
Sonja: Woher kommen Sie?
2nd Man: Aus Offenburg.
Sonja: Sind Sie hier geschäftlich?
2nd Man: Ja, ich bin zur Messe.
Sonja: Was haben Sie schon von München gesehen?
2nd Man: Den Viktualienmarkt.
Sonja: Sind Sie hier auf Geschäftsreise oder als Tourist?
3rd Man: Ich bin zur Messe hier.
Sonja: Was haben Sie schon von München gesehen?
3rd Man: Nahezu alle Sehenswürdigkeiten.
Sonja: Was machen Sie morgen?
3rd Man: Morgen geh' ich in den Englischen Garten.

A. **Alles klar?**

1. Wo ist der Marienplatz?
   a) in Dachau   b) vor dem Rathaus   c) in Schwabing

2. Was ist der Englische Garten?
   a) ein Biergarten   b) eine Messe   c) ein Park in der Stadtmitte

3. Wie viele Einwohner hat München?
   a) 1,3 Millionen   b) 3,5 Millionen   c) 2,1 Millionen

4. München ist die Hauptstadt von
   a) der BRD   b) Bayern   c) Österreich

B. **Welche Sehenswürdigkeiten gibt es in München zu sehen? Machen Sie eine Liste!**

1. ____________ 2. ____________ 3. ____________

4. ____________ 5. ____________ 6. ____________

> Although Munich is the biggest city in Bavaria, a state capital isn't always the largest city.

C. Use a map of Germany and match each **Bundesland** with its capital.

Bundesländer	**Hauptstädte**
1. Niedersachsen	______ Erfurt
2. Schleswig-Holstein	______ Düsseldorf
3. Sachsen-Anhalt	______ Stuttgart
4. Rheinland-Pfalz	______ Dresden
5. Mecklenburg-Vorpommern	______ München
6. Brandenburg	______ Lübeck
7. Bayern	______ Hannover
8. Baden-Württemberg	______ Potsdam
9. Nordrhein-Westfalen	______ Saarbrücken
10. Hessen	______ Mainz
11. Saarland	______ Magdeburg
12. Thüringen	______ Wiesbaden
13. Sachsen	______ Schwerin

Cultural Note

Although German cities share many big city problems with their American counterparts, they are not quite as crime and poverty stricken. Inner cities are generally safe for pedestrians. European cities are not as spread out as American cities. In the **Stadtmitte** (city center) is where you will find most of the large department stores and tourist attractions. Often the entire inner-city area can be covered on foot. If not, public transportation is very efficient and readily available.

D. **FÜR ZWEI**

Was haben Sie letztes Wochenende erlebt?

Find out about your partner's weekend and his/her opinion about the things he/she did. What was fun, what was boring? What was easy, what was difficult? What was healthy, what was unhealthy? You can make something up, of course!

Scene 2: Munich's Hotels

chapter 3 to 4

der Prospekt,-e brochure
Turm,¨-e tower
Vertreter,- representative
Versicherungsvertreter,- insurance sales representative

die Konferenz,-en conference
Mode fashion
Stadtrundfahrt,-en city tour
Touristenzentrale,-n tourist information, chamber of commerce
Werbeagentur,-en marketing company, advertising firm
Versicherung,-en insurance

das Stadtgründungsfest,-e Munich's anniversary celebration

ab/reisen (reist ab) to leave
an/schauen (schaut an) to see, here: to visit
betreuen to advise
ein/treffen (trifft ein), sind eingetroffen to arrive
los/schicken (schickt los) to send off
zu/schicken (schickt zu) to send

einige some
selbstverständlich sure

(Auf) Wiederhören! Bye now! (on the phone)
An welche Adresse denn? What's the address?
Könnten Sie...? could you?
mitten im Zentrum right in the center

Sandra: Hallo, ich bin Sandra, ich bin 17 Jahre alt und komme aus München.
Christine: Hallo. Ich bin Christine, und bin auch 17 Jahre alt, und wir freuen uns, daß wir euch heute unser Video über Münchner Hotels zeigen können.

Tourist Cent.: Touristenzentrale München.
Young woman: Grüß Gott. Könnten Sie mir bitte einige Prospekte über Münchner Hotels zuschicken?
Tourist Cent.: Selbstverständlich. An welche Adresse denn?
Young woman: In die Utzschneiderstr. 6 in 8 München 5.
Tourist Cent.: Ich schick' sie noch heute los.
Young woman: Gut, vielen Dank. Wiederhören.
Tourist Cent.: Wiederhören.

Christine: Die Hotelprospekte sind eingetroffen und wir schauen uns einige Hotels an.

E. **FÜR ZWEI**

Get together with a partner and use the telephone conversation above as a model to find out

a) about prices for hotel rooms
b) the hours of the **Deutsches Museum**
c) information about a guided tour of the city

> *On Screen*
>
> **München hat 33.500 Betten in 360 Hotels und Gasthöfen.**
> Munich has 33,500 beds in 360 hotels and inns.

Christine: Wir fangen mit dem Graef Hotel an. Es liegt mitten im Zentrum in der Nähe vom Viktualienmarkt.

> *On Screen*
>
> **Im Graef Hotel kostet ein Einzelzimmer zwischen 95 und 120 DM, ein Doppelzimmer zwischen 150 und 200 DM.**
> In the Graef Hotel a single room costs between 95 and 120 Marks, a double room between 150 and 200 Marks.

> *Cultural Note*
>
> When Germans answer the phone (**das Telefon**), they give their last name. Before hanging up, they say **Wiederhören!** The German phone system is not as developed as its American counterpart. For example, Germans sometimes have to wait several months until they can have a phone connected. The phone company is run by the federal post office, **die Bundespost**.

F. **Alles klar?** (Answer in complete sentences.)

1. Mit wem telefoniert Sandra?

   ____

2. Warum telefoniert Sandra?

   ____

3. Wo wohnt Sandra? Geben Sie die genaue Adresse an!

   ____

4. Wo liegt das Hotel Graef?

   ____

Grammar

In a **dependent clause** the **verb** is in **final position**. The following examples have two parts; the main clause or independent clause and the dependent clause. The main clause can stand alone. It is separated by a comma from the independent clause.

Main clause	Dependent clause
Ich weiß nicht,	**wo** das Hotel Graef **liegt.**
Sie sagt mir,	**mit wem** Sandra **telefoniert.**
Wissen Sie,	**wohin** wir gehen **müssen?**

The dependent clause can be introduced either by a conjunction:

Ich weiß, **daß** sie in einer Großstadt wohnen möchte.

or by a question word (sometimes in combination with a preposition)

Wissen Sie, **wie** ich zum Viktualienmarkt komme?
Ich weiß nicht, **an wen** ich den Brief schicken soll.

G. **FÜR ZWEI**

You have just returned from a trip to Germany. A friend wants to know everything about the country and its people. Use the questions below to form your answers.

Beispiel: **Gibt es viele Touristen in Mittenwald?**
Ich weiß, daß es in Mittenwald viele Touristen gibt.
Ich weiß nicht, ob es in Mittenwald viele Touristen gibt.

1. Liegt Mittenwald in den Bergen?
2. Wo ist der Viktualienmarkt?
3. Wo kann man einen Stadtplan bekommen?
4. Wo kann man übernachten?
5. Was kann man bei schönem Wetter in München machen?
6. Wo ist das Rathaus?
7. Wie viele Leute wohnen in München?
8. Was kann man im Englischen Garten machen?
9. Was kostet ein Zimmer in einem Hotel in der Stadtmitte?
10. Wo ist der Marienplatz?

H. FÜR ZWEI

Telefongespräch

You are planning on going to Munich and want to make reservations for a hotel room. Call up one of the hotels mentioned in the program.

- Ask if there is a room available.
- Say what kind of a room you want.
- Say how long you want to stay.
- Ask how much it will cost.

chapter 4 to 5

Scene 3: In Munich on Business

Christine: Woher kommen Sie?
Sonja: Ich komme aus Hamburg.
Christine: Sind Sie geschäftlich hier oder als Tourist?
Sonja: Ich bin geschäftlich hier — ich drehe gerade einen Film.
Christine: Was haben Sie von München schon gesehen?
Sonja: Den Marienplatz, den Viktualienmarkt und den Olympiaturm.
Christine: Was machen Sie morgen?
Sonja: Morgen geh' ich aufs Stadtgründungsfest.
Christine: Woher kommen Sie?
Man 2: Ich komme aus Osnabrück.
Christine: Sind Sie geschäftlich hier oder als Tourist?
Man 2: Ich bin hier zu einer Konferenz.

Christine: Woher kommen Sie?
Woman: Ich komme aus Düsseldorf.
Christine: Sind Sie hier geschäftlich?
Woman: Ich bin zur Modemesse hier.
Christine: Was haben Sie schon von München gesehen?

Woman: Ich habe gestern eine Stadtrundfahrt gemacht und habe sehr viele Sehenswürdigkeiten schon gesehen.
Christine: Was machen Sie morgen?
Woman: Morgen muß ich leider wieder abreisen.

Cultural Note

Das City Hilton hat zwei Restaurants und ein Café. Es hat 483 Zimmer, 20 Juniorsuiten und eine Präsidentensuite.
The City Hilton has two restaurants and a café. It has 483 rooms, 20 junior suites and a presidential suite.

I. **Listen and answer the following questions:**

1. Woher kommen die Leute?

   a. ______________________________

   b. ______________________________

   c. ______________________________

2. Sind sie als Touristen in München?

   ____

3. Was machen die Leute geschäftlich in München?

   a. ______________________________

   b. ______________________________

   c. ______________________________

München ist weltbekannt (world famous) **für die vielen Messen, die hier stattfinden** (take place). **Vielleicht kommt ihr auch zuerst als Geschäftsleute und nicht als Touristen hierher.**

J. **FÜR ZWEI**

Warum? Use the suggestions given below or any ideas of your own you may wish to add. Explain why you would do the following things in the format shown below.

Beispiel: Warum gehst du auf den Viktualienmarkt?
Ich gehe auf den Viktualienmarkt, weil ich Obst und Gemüse kaufen will.

1. Warum möchtest du München besuchen?
   a. Es gibt viele Messen.
   b. Es gibt viele Sehenswürdigkeiten.
   c. Ich möchte die Biergärten besuchen.
   d. ?

2. Warum möchtest du in einer Jugendherberge übernachten?
   a. Die Hotels sind zu teuer.
   b. Man trifft da viele interessante Leute.
   c. Es gibt keinen Campingplatz in der Stadtmitte.
   d. ?

3. Warum gehst du zur Touristenzentrale?
    a. Ich brauche einen Stadtplan
    b. Dort kann man Hotelprospekte bekommen.
    c. Dort kann ich bayrisch sprechen.
    d. ?

4. Warum gehst du in einen Biergarten?
    a. Ich trinke gern Bier.
    b. Das Wetter ist schön.
    c. Mein Zimmer ist klein und dunkel.
    d. ?

5. Warum möchtest du gern in einer Großstadt wohnen?
    a. Es ist viel los.
    b. Man kann in Konzerte, Museen und Theater gehen.
    c. Das Leben ist dort interessanter.
    d. ?

K **Und Sie? Möchten Sie lieber als Tourist oder geschäftlich nach München reisen? Was würden Sie in München machen?** Write ten sentences about a prospective trip to Munich. Start each sentence with: **Ich würde...**

Scene 4: At a Trade Fair

chapter 5 to 6

On Screen

Jedes Jahr finden hier 17 Messen und 48 Kongresse statt. Die ISPO ist eine internationale Fachmesse für Sportartikel und Sportmode. 1360 Firmen aus 35 Ländern beteiligen sich.

Every year 17 trade fairs and 48 conventions take place here. ISPO is a special international fair for sports equipment and sports fashion in which 1360 companies from 35 countries participate.

Sonja: Wie heißt du?
Paul: Ich heiße Paul.
Sonja: Woher kommst du?
Paul: Aus England.
Sonja: Sprichst du Deutsch?
Paul: Ich verstehe so viel, aber spreche nur ein bißchen.
Sonja: Ist es schwer, Deutsch zu lernen?
Paul: Ja, ein bißchen, manchmal.

Sonja: Woher kommen Sie?
Barbara: Ich komme aus den Vereinigten Staaten, aus Texas.
Sonja: Sprechen Sie Deutsch?
Barbara: Ja, ich spreche Deutsch.
Sonja: Seit wann sprechen Sie Deutsch?
Barbara: Ich spreche Deutsch seit 15 Jahren.
Sonja: Und war es schwer, Deutsch zu lernen?
Barbara: Ja, Deutsch ist eine sehr schwierige Sprache.
Sonja: Brauchen Sie die Fremdsprache für Ihren Beruf?
Barbara: Ja, ich muß ja Deutsch sprechen jeden Tag und weil ich hier lebe, und außerdem bin ich hier auf der ISPO und meistens zweimal im Jahr, und da muß ich ja Deutsch sprechen.

L. **Fill in the blanks as you watch the video.**

1. Wie lange sprechen sie schon Deutsch?

   Barbara: ________________ Amanda: ________________ Vicky: ________________

2. Warum sprechen Barbara, Amanda und Vicky Deutsch?

   ____

M. **Und Sie?** Answer the following questions about yourself, and write down the answer.

1. Seit wann lernen Sie Deutsch?

____

2. Ist es schwer, Deutsch zu lernen?

____

3. Warum lernen Sie Deutsch?

____

Some impersonal expressions are followed by **zu** (to).

Es war schwer, Deutsch zu lernen.
It was difficult to learn German.

Here are some other examples:

Es macht Spaß,...	It's fun...	**zu schwimmen.** to swim.
Es ist schön,...	It's beautiful...	**nicht arbeiten zu müssen.** not to have to work.
Es ist nötig,...	It's necessary...	
Es ist langweilig,...	It's boring...	**Geld zu verdienen.** to earn money.
Es ist gefährlich,...	It's dangerous...	
Es ist (un)gesund,...	It's (un)healthy...	
Es ist teuer/billig...	It's expensive/cheap...	

N. **FÜR ZWEI**

Ask each other the following questions. Use the infinitive with **zu** in the answers.

1. Was macht Spaß?
2. Was ist gefährlich?
3. Was ist gesund?
4. Was ist teuer?
5. Was ist langweilig?

O. **FÜR ZWEI ODER GRUPPEN: Wann braucht man Deutsch?**

For situations in which you might need German, write sentences that match the drawings.

Scene 5: At a Street Festival

chapter 6 to 7

der **Geburtstag,-e** birthday
Hafen,- harbor
Jugendliche,-n teenager, adolescent
See,-n lake

die **Gründung,-en** founding
Sache,-n thing
Welt,-en world
Weltstadt,¨-e metropolis

das **Fest,-e** party, celebration
Gebäude,- building
Klima climate

sich erinnern an to remember
surfen to surf
weg/gehen (geht weg) to go out

als Jugendlicher as a teenager/adolescent
aus dem Ausland from abroad
diese ganzen Sachen all these things
eigentlich schon/nicht actually yes/not
es ist (nicht) viel los there is (not) much going on

> **unheimlich** is often used in connection with other adjectives, e.g., **unheimlich schön/nett/teuer/viel.** In this context it is colloquial and means very beautiful/nice/expensive/ much.

Sonja: Erinnert ihr euch an den Hafengeburtstag in Hamburg? Auch München feiert, wie z. B. das Stadtgründungsfest.

> *On Screen*
>
> **München, benannt nach den Benediktiner-Mönchen, die dort lebten, wurde im Jahre 1158 von Heinrich dem Löwen gegründet.**
> Munich, named after the Benedictine monks who lived there, was founded in the year 1158 by Henry the Lion.

Sonja: München ist wirklich eine Weltstadt mit vielen Touristen aus dem Ausland. Aber leben die Münchner selbst gern hier? Ich fragte einige: Lebst du gern in München?

Luca: Ja, ich lebe sehr gern in München. Ich mag das Klima, die Leute, einfach alles.
Sonja: Lebst du gern in München?
Tina: Ja.
Sonja: Warum?
Tina: Weil es gibt hier unheimlich viele Theater, Kinos, Tanzschulen und diese ganzen Sachen, und man kann unheimlich viel als Jugendlicher hier machen.

Sonja: Lebst du gern in München?
Florian: Eigentlich nicht, denn München ist eine recht langweilige Stadt.
Sonja: Was kann man hier als Jugendlicher machen?
Florian: Man kann abends weggehen, man kann in 'n Biergarten gehen, man kann surfen gehen—wir haben viele Seen—, aber sonst ist nicht sehr viel los hier in München.

Sonja: Was kann man in München machen?
Klaus: Einiges. Man kann Museen besuchen, Konzerte, ins Kino gehen, Theater.
Sonja: Und was machst du dieses Wochenende?
Klaus: Ich werd' zum Stadtgründungsfest gehen.

Sonja: Lebst du gern in München?
Verena: Ja, eigentlich schon.
Sonja: Und warum?
Verena: Weil es eine schöne Stadt ist. Man kann sich Gebäude anschauen, in Museen gehen. Es gibt schöne Biergärten und Parks.

Sonja: Lebst du gern in München?
Vanessa: Nein, ich leb' nicht gern in München.
Sonja: Warum nicht?
Vanessa: Es ist mir zu langweilig hier.

Jan: Ja, ich leb' sehr gern in München. Es ist so schön grün hier, und es ist eine einfach schöne Stadt.

P. **Leben die Münchner gern in ihrer Stadt? Schreiben Sie warum oder warum nicht!**

1. Luca lebt gern in München, weil ______________________________

   ____

2. Tina ______________________________

   ____

3. Florian ______________________________

   ____

4. Verena ______________________________

   ____

5. Vanessa ______________________________

   ____

Q. **FÜR ZWEI**

<u>**In München**</u>

Sie sind letzten Sommer als Tourist in München gewesen. Combine one element from each column to tell your partner what you have done in the Bavarian capital. Change the infinitives to the past participle.

Beispiel: **Letzten Sommer habe ich den Englischen Garten an<u>ge</u>sehen.**

Letzten Sommer...
Am ersten Tag...
Am ersten Abend...
Dann...
Am Wochenende...
Bei schönem Wetter hat mein/e Freund/in...
Am nächsten Tag...

bin ich	**den Englischen Garten ansehen.**
habe ich	**das Deutsche Museum besuchen.**
haben meine Freunde und ich	**in den Biergarten gehen.**
sind meine Freunde und ich	**im Hotel übernachten.**
ist mein/e Freund/in	**_?_ essen.**
	_?_ lesen.
	_?_ fahren.
	_?_ sehen.
	_?_ besuchen.

R. **FÜR ZU HAUSE: Written Exercise**

Was wissen Sie über München? Write a short paragraph. Talk about the history of the city, its size, and its population, what there is to see and do (sights, annual events, entertainment). What do people from Munich think about their city? Why do people go there?

PROGRAMM 14

WIR TREIBEN SPORT

This episode is devoted to sports, whether it is high performance athletics, a weekend spectacle, a team game, or an individual fitness training and leisure activity. We visit a soccer match in the Munich Sports Stadium, and also learn what people of different age groups like about sports. We also meet one of Germany's most promising ice skaters.

Sonja beim Tae-Kwon-Do

LANGUAGE FUNCTIONS

- talking about leisure activities
- stating personal reasons
- more on expressing ease/difficulty
- saying what you like and dislike

CONTENTS

- sports and fitness
- habits
- health and the body
- relative clauses

chapter 7 to 14

Scene 1: At a Soccer Match in the Munich Sports Stadium

chapter 8 to 9

der Angriffsfußball aggressive soccer
Deutsche Meister national champion
Fan,-s fan
Fußball soccer
Sitzplatz,¨-e seat
Stehplatz,¨-e standing room
Verein,-e team, club
Wettkampf,¨-e competition, track meet

die Bundesliga national major league
Leichtathletik track and field
Sicherheit,-en certainty, safety
Sportart,-en sports discipline

das Bundesligaspiel,-e game in the national major league

aus/tragen (trägt aus) to carry out
siegen = gewinnen to win
statt/finden (findet statt) takes place

halt is a filler word that is often used in colloquial spoken German. It generally means "you know" and one should refrain from using it too often.

Cultural Note

Fußball is by far Germany's most popular team game. Every Saturday evening millions of Germans eagerly wait for the **Sportschau**, a German TV program where they can watch reports on the most important **Bundesligaspiele**, major league games, and are informed about all the results. There are twenty major league teams in the **Fußballbundesliga**. The two most prominent teams mentioned in this episode are **Bayern München** and **Borussia Dortmund**.

Sonja: Die Olympischen Spiele von 1972 wurden hier in München ausgetragen. In diesem Stadion fanden die Leichtathletikwettkämpfe statt.

> ***On Screen***
>
> **Es waren die ersten Olympischen Spiele in Deutschland seit 1936.**
> They were the first Olympic games in Germany since 1936.

A. **Alles klar?**

1. Wann wurden die Olympischen Spiele in München ausgetragen?

   a) 1974 b) 1972 c) 1970

2. Bayern München ist ein

   a) Leichtathletikverein b) Fußballfan c) ein Fußballverein

3. Wer wird das Bundesligaspiel gewinnen? Was glauben die Leute aus Dortmund?

   a) der AC Mailand b) Borussia Dortmund c) Bayern München

4. Wer wurde Deutscher Meister?

   a) der AC Mailand b) Borussia Dortmund c) Bayern München

B. **Beantworten Sie folgende Fragen zum Film!** (Write one sentence for each question.)

1. Warum sind Tausende von Fußballfans ins Stadion gekommen?

   ____

2. Wie finden die Jugendlichen aus München ihren Verein?

   ____

3. Welcher Verein hat das Fußballspiel gewonnen?

   ____

C. **Und Sie? Gehen Sie auch manchmal zu einer Sportveranstaltung** (sports event)? **Für welche Sportart interessieren Sie sich?** Write three sentences expressing your interest in sports events.

Scene 2: What Sports Teenagers Like

der Baseballhandschuh,-e baseball glove
Baseballschläger,- baseball bat
Helm,-e helmet

das Aerobics aerobics
Baseball the sport of baseball
Eishockey ice hockey
Segel,- sail
Segeln sailing
Surfbrett,-er surfboard
Surfen surfing
Tae-Kwon-Do

die Ausrüstung,-en equipment

segeln to sail
sich verteidigen to defend oneself
trainieren to exercise
zu/gucken (guckt zu) = zu/schauen (schaut zu) to watch

außerdem besides, on top of that
profihaft as a professional
super great

eine Sportart treiben to engage in a sports activity
unter der Woche during the week
wenn's ginge if it were possible

Sonja: Vielen Jugendlichen macht es genauso viel Spaß, eine Sportart zu treiben wie anderen beim Sport zuzugucken. Ich fragte sie: Welche Sportart treibst du?

Georg: Ich mache Tae-Kwon-Do.
Sonja: Und wie oft?
Georg: Ein bis zweimal die Woche.
Sonja: Was gefällt dir daran?
Georg: Ja, da lernt man sich zu verteidigen, und außerdem sind die Leute da super.
Sandra: Ich geh' zum Tanzen und ab und zu zu Aerobic.
Sonja: Wie oft gehst du in die Tanzschule?
Sandra: Einmal die Woche.
Sonja: Was macht dir daran Spaß?
Sandra: Daß man neue Leute kennenlernt und einfach das Tanzen.

D. As you watch the video, have a pencil ready and write down the desired information in the spaces provided below.

Welche Sportart(en) treiben ...?

a) Georg ______________________________

b) Sandra ______________________________

c) Luca ______________________________

d) Klaus ______________________________

e) Jan ______________________________

Wie oft trainieren sie?

a) Georg ______________________________

b) Sandra ______________________________

c) Luca ______________________________

d) Klaus ______________________________

e) Jan ______________________________

Welche Ausrüstung brauchen sie?

a) Luca ______________________________

b) Klaus ______________________________

Grammar

Relative pronouns (in English "that," "which," "who," "whose," "whom") are identical with the definite article, except for the dative plural and the genitive forms. They introduce dependent clauses and refer to an *antecedent* in the main clause (either a person or a thing that is previously mentioned).

Is this the player **who** had an accident?
This is the team **which** we like a lot.

	Masculine	Feminine	Neuter	Plural
Nominative	der	die	das	die
Accusative	den	die	das	die
Dative	dem	der	dem	denen
Genitive	dessen	deren	dessen	deren

Relative pronouns agree in gender and number with their antecedent (the person or thing previously mentioned to which they refer).

Beispiele:

Das ist **ein Hobby, das** sehr viel Spaß macht. (**Nom.**)
Basketball ist **ein Sport, den** man bei jedem Wetter treiben kann (**Acc.**).
Das ist **die Studentin, mit der** ich immer Tennis spiele (**Dat.**)
Das sind **die Fußballfans, deren** Verein verloren hat. (**Gen.**)
Eiskunstlauf ist **der einzigste Sport, der** das Sportliche mit der Kreativität verbindet. (**Nom.**)
(Ice skating is the only sport that combines athletics with creativity.)
Tae-Kwon-Do ist **eine Sportart, in der** nicht nur der Körper geschult wird. **(Dat.)**

E. **FÜR ZWEI**

Define for your partner the following by using a relative clause.

Beispiel: Was ist Paris? - Paris ist eine Stadt, die in Frankreich liegt.

1. Paris
2. Picasso
3. Fußball
4. Tae-Kwon-Do
5. Arnold Schwarzenegger
6. Schlafanzug
7. Mensa
8. Jugendherberge
9. Baseball
10. München
11. Bayern
12. Viktualienmarkt
13. Mittenwald
14. Surfbrett
15. Schlittschuh
16. Borussia Dortmund

F. **FÜR GRUPPEN: Zeichnen & Raten.**

One student draws a picture of sports equipment. The others try to name the sport to which it belongs. Everyone gets a chance to be an artist!

Scene 3: Julia Buckley, Ice Skating Champion

chapter 10 to 11

der **Ort,-e** town
Profi,-s professional

die **Kreativität,-en** creativity
Kür,-en free skating
Siegerehrung,-en award ceremony
Trainerin,-nen female trainer

das **Eiskunstlaufen** ice skating
Sportliche here: athletics

im ersten Stock on the second floor (first floor above the ground floor)

verbinden to combine

Julia:	Ich heiße Julia Buckley und bin 15 Jahre alt. Ich lebe in Garmisch-Partenkirchen. In meiner Freizeit gehe ich gern durch unseren Ort.
	Mein größtes Hobby ist Eiskunstlaufen. Ich trainiere jeden Tag 2 Stunden lang. Meine Trainerin ist immer dabei. Es macht unheimlich viel Spaß, draußen in der Sonne Schlittschuh zu laufen. Meine Mutter guckt mir zu.
	Dies ist unser Haus. Mein Zimmer liegt im ersten Stock. Hier mache ich meine Hausaufgaben. Mein Lieblingsfach ist Englisch. Hier bin ich bei einer Siegerehrung in Italien.
	Mein Vater ist Amerikaner aus New York. Er ist Geschäftsmann. Meine Mutter ist Deutsche. Sie ist Lehrerin hier in Garmisch. Hier tanze ich meine Kür.
Sonja:	Wie oft trainierst du in der Woche?
Julia:	Jeden Tag 2 Stunden.
Sonja:	Was gefällt dir besonders an diesem Sport?
Julia:	Es ist der einzigste Sport, der das Sportliche mit der Kreativität verbindet.
Sonja:	Es sieht so leicht aus. Ist es schwer?
Julia:	Ja, es ist sehr schwer, und es braucht sehr viel Training, bis es eben so leicht aussieht.
Sonja:	Und möchtest du später Profi werden?
Julia:	Ja.

G. Fill out the questionnaire about Julia and her family.

Name: Julia Buckley ______________________

Alter: ________ **Wohnort:** ______________________

Hobbys: ______________________ ______________________

Beruf: ______________________

Lieblingsfach: ______________________

Beruf des Vaters: ______________________

Beruf der Mutter: ______________________

H. **FÜR ZWEI: Interview**

Geht es Ihnen gut? You are a doctor and have to give advice to one of your patients. Interview your partner about personal habits and health. After filling out the questionnaire, discuss your partner's health with her/him.

1. Alter: ____________________
2. Körpergröße: ____________ cm
3. Gewicht: ______________ Kilo
4. männlich ______ weiblich ______
5. Beruf: ______________________

Mein Beruf und mein Alltag	**richtig**	**falsch**
6. Mein Beruf macht mir Spaß	____	____
7. Es gibt viel Streß in meinem Leben	____	____
8. Ich schlafe genug	____	____
9. Ich habe viele Freunde	____	____
10. Meine Freunde und Familie verstehen mich gut	____	____
11. Ich bin nervös und kann mich nicht entspannen	____	____
12. Ich sage immer, was ich denke	____	____
13. Ich habe zu wenig Freizeit	____	____

Sportliche Aktivitäten	**richtig**	**falsch**
14. Ich treibe Sport	____	____
15. Ich treibe mindestens einmal die Woche Sport	____	____

Schwimmen ____ Skilaufen ____ Tennis

Radfahren ____ Fußball ____ Aerobics

Basketball ____ Gymnastik ____ Anderes

16. Ich bin Mitglied eines Sportvereins	____	____
17. Ich bin Leistungssportler/in	____	____

Meine Lebensgewohnheiten		richtig	falsch
18.	Ich esse gern Fleisch	______	______
19.	Ich esse oft Kuchen, Schokolade oder Süßigkeiten	______	______
20.	Ich trinke oft Alkohol	______	______
21.	Ich trinke manchmal Alkohol	______	______
22.	Ich rauche	______	______
23.	Ich habe früher geraucht	______	______
24.	Ich trinke viel Kaffee	______	______

Write an essay of about 15-20 sentences relating to your habits and their effect on your health.

Scene 4: Practicing Tae-Kwon-Do

chapter 11 to 12

> *On Screen*
>
> **TAE = mit dem Fuß schlagen, KWON = mit der Hand u. Faust schlagen, DO = der geistige Weg.**
> TAE = to strike with the foot, KWON = to strike with hand or fist, DO = the spiritual way.

der **Körper,-** body
Geist spirit
Gurt,-e belt

die **Kampfsportart,-en** martial arts
Schutzausrüstung,-en protective suit

aus/probieren (probiert aus) to try out
kämpfen to fight
schulen to train
stärken to strengthen

das **Jiu Jutsu**
Selbstbewußtsein self esteem, self confidence

abwechslungsreich interesting, varied
beweglich flexible

das verkrafte ich schon I can handle that
es hält fit it keeps you fit
Was reizt dich an dieser Sportart? What do you find appealing about this sport?

Sonja: Zuhause habe ich dreimal pro Woche Jiu Jutsu. Ich trainiere zwei Stunden sehr hart, und ich mag es, weil es fit hält.
Heute möchte ich eine neue Kampfsportart ausprobieren — Tae-Kwon-Do.

(Interview with Thomas, teacher of Tae-Kwon-Do.)

Sonja: Seit wann machst du Tae-Kwon-Do?
Thomas: Ich mach' Tae-Kwon-Do seit 13 Jahren und bin seit 8 Jahren Trainer.
Sonja: Was reizt dich gerade an dieser Sportart?
Thomas: Tae-Kwon-Do ist eine Sportart, in der nicht nur der Körper geschult wird, sondern auch der Geist.
Sonja: Kann jeder Tae-Kwon-Do machen?

Thomas: Tae-Kwon-Do kann jeder machen. Vom 6. bis zum 57. Lebensjahr haben wir Schüler in unserem Verein.
Sonja: Seit wann machst du Tae-Kwon-Do?
Christian: Seit 2 Jahren.
Sonja: Wie oft trainierst du?
Christian: Sechsmal in der Woche.
Sonja: Sechsmal? Ist das nicht etwas viel?
Christian: Nee, das verkrafte ich schon.

Sonja: Wie oft kommst du hierher?
Ellen: Zweimal die Woche.
Sonja: Geht da nicht viel von deiner Freizeit ab?
Ellen: Doch schon, aber es macht Spaß.
Sonja: Was gefällt dir besonders an dem Sport?
Ellen: Es hält fit, und es macht halt Spaß und stärkt das Selbstbewußtsein.
Sonja: Könntest du dich gegen einen Mann verteidigen?
Ellen: Ich glaub' schon, ja.

Sonja: Was für eine Ausrüstung brauchst du?
Claudia: Ich brauch' erstmal den Anzug, dann den Gurt, und später, also wenn ich kämpfen möchte, dann brauch' ich eine Schutzausrüstung.
Sonja: Wieviel kostet alles zusammen?
Claudia: Ungefähr 90 Mark.
Sonja: Was gefällt dir besonders am Tae-Kwon-Do?
Claudia: Man wird sehr beweglich; es ist abwechslungsreich, man denkt, daß man sich verteidigen kann, hat mehr Selbsbewußtsein.

I. **Alles klar?**

1. Was ist Jiu Jutsu?

   a) ein chinesisches Nudelgericht b) ein neuer Tanz c) eine Kampfsportart

2. Wie lange macht Thomas schon Tae-Kwon-Do?

   a) seit acht Jahren b) seit 13 Jahren c) seit dem 6. Lebensjahr

3. Was reizt (gefällt) Thomas an Tae-Kwon-Do?

   a) Daß es jeder machen kann.
   b) Daß es neu ist.
   c) Daß nicht nur der Körper, sondern auch der Geist geschult wird.

4. Seit wann macht Christian Tae-Kwon-Do?

   a) seit dem 57. Lebensjahr b) seit zwei Jahren c) seit 13 Jahren

J. **Answer the following questions.**

1. Wie oft macht Ellen Tae-Kwon-Do?

   ____

2. Was gefällt Ellen besonders an dieser Sportart?

   ____

3. Was für eine Ausrüstung braucht man für Tae-Kwon-Do?

   ____

4. Ist Tae-Kwo-Do eine teuere Sportart?

   ____

5. Was gefällt Claudia besonders an dieser Sportart?

   ____

K. **FÜR ZWEI ODER GRUPPEN**

Fußball - Football - was ist anders, ähnlich, gleich? Talk with your partner(s) about Spielregeln, Ausrüstung, Fans, etc. Was gefällt Ihnen besser? Warum?

chapter 12 to 13

Scene 5: At a "Faustball" Game

der Faustball,¨-e fistball
Mannschaftsgeist = Teamgeist team spirit
Punktspieltag,-e day of competition

die Faust,¨-e fist
Halle,-n gym
Mannschaft,-en team

das Punktspiel,-e playing for points
Trikot,-s sports jersey

betreiben = treiben to do
sich verletzen to hurt oneself

im Freien outdoors
Wie bist du darauf gekommen? How did you get the idea?

> ### *Cultural Note*
>
> In the 1970s the **Deutsche Sportbund** (German Sports Federation) responded to alarming evidence that too many West Germans did not engage in any kind of physical activity, and that health, endurance and life expectancy were compromised by neglect of physical fitness. A national campaign was launched and by the 1980s millions of citizens had joined the **Trimm-Dich-Bewegung** (physical fitness movement).

L. **Listen and fill in the blanks.**

Sonja:	Was gefällt dir am Faustball?
Gerhard:	Der Mannschaftsgeist.
Sonja:	Wie bist du darauf gekommen?
Gerhard:	Durch meinen ____________________ .
Sonja:	Was ist ein Faustball?
Gerhard:	Ein Faustball ist so ähnlich wie ein ____________________, nur schwerer.

Sonja: Was für eine Sportart treiben Sie?

Jürgen: Ich spiele ________________________.
Sonja: Und wie oft?
Jürgen: Zweimal die ________________________.
Sonja: Wann spielen Sie Faustball?
Jürgen: Wir spielen Faustball mittwochs und ________________________ abends nach der Uni.
Sonja: Was gefällt Ihnen an dieser Sportart?
Jürgen: Besonders gefällt mir der Teamgeist und daß man den Sport im

________________________ betreiben kann.
Sonja: Was gefällt dir am Faustball?

Ralf: Es ist ein sehr fairer________________________; man kann sich wenig verletzen.
Sonja: Ist es ein teurer Sport?
Ralf: Also für uns ist es nicht ________________________; wir müssen nur die Trikots zahlen; das ist 50 Mark.
Sonja: Kann man es auch im Winter spielen?

Ralf: Wir spielen's im ________________________, da spielen wir in der Halle und

es macht sehr viel________________________.
Sonja: Was für einen Sport treiben Sie?

Konrad: Ich ________________________ Faustball.
Sonja: Wie oft trainieren Sie?
Konrad: Ich trainiere ca. zwei-dreimal die Woche und jedes ________________________ dann ein Punktspieltag.

M. <u>Alles klar</u>? Schreiben Sie 5-10 Sätze und erklären Sie einem/r Freund/in, was Faustball ist.

N. **FÜR ZWEI ODER GRUPPEN: Ferien und Fitness**

A new hotel has opened that offers a special vacation program for people who want to get back in shape. You are asked to write a short description for a brochure. First discuss with your partner(s) what a place like that should offer. Talk about location, sports, diet, entertainment, costs and what a daily routine should be like. Then write the description. Keep it short.

Scene 6: Teens Practicing Gymnastics

der Leistungsreiz,-e challenge
Reiz,-e appeal, attraction

die Leistung,-en accomplishment, achievement

Puma the name of a German sporting goods company

sich etwas aus/denken (denkt sich etwas aus) to think up something
teil/nehmen (nimmt teil) to participate
turnen to do gymastics

vielfältig diverse, interesting

das Gerät,-e piece of apparatus
Kunstturnen gymnastics

Cultural Note

Many Germans are members of a **Sportverein** (sports club). There are now over 50,000 **Vereine** nationally, and nearly one out of four Germans has joined one of the clubs, which not only participate in local and regional competition, but also serve as community centers for social gatherings. The tradition of the **Sportvereine** goes back to the nineteenth century, when these organizations frequently also had a secret political agenda.

Sonja: Was für eine Sportart treibst du?
Uschi: Ich turne.
Sonja: Und wie oft trainierst du?
Uschi: Ich gehe zwei- bis dreimal ins Training.
Sonja: Was gefällt dir an diesem Sport?
Uschi: Der Leistungsreiz und die Wettkämpfe.

Sonja: Was für Sport machst du?
Ilona: Ich mache Kunstturnen.
Sonja: Wie oft gehst du zum Training?
Ilona: Ich trainiere dreimal die Woche.
Sonja: Seit wann turnst du schon?
Ilona: Ich turne, seitdem ich 6 Jahre alt bin.
Sonja: Und was gefällt dir besonders am Turnen?
Ilona: Turnen macht mir Spaß, besonders weil's so vielfältig ist, weil man sich selbst Übungen ausdenken kann, weil's verschiedene Geräte gibt.
Sonja: Möchtest du später einmal Profi werden?
Ilona: Nein, aber ich nehm' oft an Shows teil, wie z.B. auf der ISPO-Show für Puma.

O. **FÜR ZWEI**

Was ist (un)gesund? Rate each activity in Column A for its impact on the items in Column B. Use the adjectives in Column C in your ratings.

A		B	C
Tae-Kwon-Do		das Herz	
Schwimmen		die Lunge	
Rauchen		das Selbstbewußtsein	
Faustball		den Geist	gut
Turnen		die Beine	gesund
Streß	ist für	die Augen	ungesund
Aerobics		den Körper	schlecht
Radfahren		die Füße	
Skilaufen		den Bauch	
Eiskunstlaufen		den Rücken	
Lesen		die Arme	
?		?	

P. **FÜR EINE/N, ZWEI ODER MEHRERE: Vier Sportler**

Welche Sportarten treiben sie?

Hansi:
Er ist 16 Jahre alt. Sein Vorbild ist Franz Beckenbauer. Er trainiert dreimal in der Woche mit seinen Kameraden vom Sportverein. Hansi steht am liebsten im Tor, aber sein Trainer sagt, er müsse seine Beinarbeit noch verbessern. Später möchte er in der Bundesliga spielen.

Jürgen:
Er ist 57 Jahre alt, sieht aber 10 Jahre jünger aus. Er ist ausgeglichen, fit und beweglich. Das alles verdankt er der Sportart, die er seit 15 Jahren ausübt. Beim Training trägt er einen weißen Anzug und einen schwarzen Gürtel.

Sibille:
Sie ist 17 Jahre alt, meistens ziemlich braun und hat eine Idealfigur. Ihren Sport übt sie ausschließlich im Freien aus. Zu ihrer Ausrüstung gehören ein Brett mit Segel und ein Gummianzug. Nach dem Abitur möchte Sibille nach Hawaii ziehen, weil sie dort das ganze Jahr trainieren kann.

Erwin:
Er ist 19 Jahre alt, groß und hat einen muskulösen Oberkörper. Seit kurzem trägt er eine Glatze, damit er in seinem Sport noch schneller ist. Erwin ist der beste Krauler seiner Mannschaft. "Unglaublich", sagt seine Mutter, "als Kind hat er nämlich gar nicht gern gebadet!"

PROGRAMM 15

DU BIST, WAS DU ISST

This episode deals with food. Not only do we learn about German eating and drinking habits, but we also discuss the nutritional value of certain foods. We visit a German **Konditorei**, where Sonja interviews a variety of people who talk about their food preferences.

Der Viktualienmarkt

LANGUAGE FUNCTIONS

- expressing food preferences
- evaluating, judging
- talking about food, exercise, and physical health
- talking about physical activity
- asking about prices

CONTENTS

- diet and eating habits
- German food and drink
- health and fitness
- adjective endings

chapter 1 to 9

Scene 1: What People Eat

chapter 2 to 3

der **Alkohol** alcohol
Hamburger,- hamburger
Kuchen,- cake, pie
Salat,-e salad

die **Butter,-** butter
Erdbeere,-n strawberry
Kalorie,-n calorie
Schale,-n bowl
Schokolade chocolate
Süßigkeit,-en candy
Torte,-n layer cake, torte
Zigarette,-n cigarette

das **Eis** ice cream
Fast Food
Fleisch meat
Gemüse (sing.) vegetables
Nahrungsmittel,- food
Obst (sing.) fruit
Sojaprodukt,-e soy product
Vitamin,-e vitamin
Vollkornprodukt,-e whole grain product

dick fat, obese (people)
fett greasy, fat (food)
mager lean, skinny
scharf spicy, hot
schlank slender, thin (people)
schmecken to taste
vegetarisch vegetarian

Sonja: In dieser Folge geht es ums Essen. Durch welche Nahrungsmittel bleibt man schlank und gesund — was macht dick und ist ungesund?
This episode deals with food. Which foods keep you slim and healthy—and which ones are fattening and unhealthy?

(Buying strawberries at a market stall.)
Eine Schale Erdbeeren, bitte.
Nehmen wir die, die sind schön.

Clerk: 3 Mark, bitte.

Sonja: Ich esse viel Obst und Gemüse. Ich finde, es schmeckt gut und ist sehr gesund. Ich fragte: Was soll man essen — was ist gesund?

Monika: Ja viel Obst und Gemüse.
Sonja: Und was meinst du sollte man möglichst nicht essen?
Monika: Süßigkeiten, Kuchen, Eis — alles was schmeckt.

Sonja: Was ist gesundes Essen?
Bernd: Obst, Gemüse, Fisch, Sojaprodukte, Vollkornprodukte...

Sonja: Was sollte man essen?
Miriam: Ja, Sachen mit weniger Kalorien und also Obst recht viel, Vitamine und so.
Sonja: Und was ist ungesund?
Miriam: Ja so Fast Food, also Hamburger und, oder Torten.

Sonja: Was sollte man vermeiden?
Petra: Fettes Essen, viel Fleisch und Alkohol.

Tina: Schokolade, Alkohol, Zigaretten.

Sonja: Welche Nahrungsmittel sind gesund?
Thomas: Also Salate natürlich mit viel Vitaminen und sonst wenig Fleisch und alles in der Richtung, also mehr vegetarisch.

Sonja: Was sollte man nicht essen?
Rina: Ja Süßigkeiten, also Schokolade und Fleisch und Butter.

A. **Machen Sie eine Liste!**

Was ist gesund?	**Was ist ungesund?**
______________________	______________________
______________________	______________________
______________________	______________________
______________________	______________________
______________________	______________________
______________________	______________________
______________________	______________________

Grammar Note

Remember the adjective endings without a preceding **der**-word or **ein**-word.

	der Wein	die Schokolade	das Essen	die Erdbeeren
Nom.	deutsch**er**	süß**e**	fettig**es**	frisch**e**
Acc.	deutsch**en**	süß**e**	fettig**es**	frisch**e**
Dat.	deutsch**em**	süß**er**	fettig**em**	frisch**en**

Example: Das ist deutsch**er** Wein. **oder:** Ich trinke deutsch**en** Wein. **oder:** Fettig**es** Essen ist ungesund. Schokoladeneis mit frisch**en** Erdbeeren schmeckt, aber macht leider dick.

B. **FÜR ZWEI**

Was essen Sie gern? Was interessiert Sie? Describe what you like and what you don't like. Use adjectives to describe the things you like. Talk to your partner about your preferences.

Beispiel: Italienisches Essen schmeckt mir. Ich esse gerne in italienischen Restaurants.

italienisch-	**Leute**		
süß-	**Städte**		
mexikanisch-	**Restaurants**		
deutsch-	**Kuchen**		
französisch-	**Bier**	**interessiert**	**mich**
frisch-	**Wein**	**interessieren**	
fettig-	**Obst**		
gesund-	**Gericht**		
mager-	**Brot**	**schmeckt**	**mir**
exotisch-	**Fleisch**	**schmecken**	
indisch-	**Essen**		
europäisch-			
chinesisch-			
scharf-			
kalt-			

Scene 2: Eating Between Meals

chapter 3 to 4

der Joghurt,-s yoghurt
Müsliriegel,- cereal bar

die Kleinigkeit,-en small thing
Mahlzeit,-en meal

sich ernähren to eat
vermeiden to avoid
widerstehen to withstand (temptation)
Dieser Kuchen steckt voller Fett. This cake is full of fat.
genau wie ich just like me
lecker delicious

> *On Screen*
>
> **Hier sucht man sich einen Kuchen und bekommt einen Zettel. Dann setzt man sich und gibt den Zettel der Bedienung, die den Kuchen bringt.**
> Here you select a piece of cake and you get a piece of paper. Then you sit down and hand the piece of paper to the waitress who brings you the cake.

(Sonja orders a cake at counter.)

Sonja: Also Erdbeerschnitte.
Clerk: Danke Ihnen.
Sonja: Hm. Lecker. Genau das was ich gerade tue, sollte man vermeiden, wenn man sich gesund ernähren möchte. Dieser Kuchen steckt voller Fett, Kalorien und Zucker, aber er schmeckt fantastisch. Viele Leute können genau wie ich nicht widerstehen. Ich fragte: Ißt du zwischen den Mahlzeiten?

C. <u>Alles klar</u>? Listen to the people Sonja interviews and make a list of things they eat in between meals.

Was essen sie zwischen den Mahlzeiten?

Shamin: ______________________________

Luca: ______________________________

Nicole: ______________________________

Petra: ______________________________

Scene 3: What People Eat For Breakfast

der Aufschnitt sliced meat and sausage
Fruchtsaft,⁻e fruit juice
Kakao cocoa
Quark milk product similar to cottage cheese
Vegetarier,- vegetarian

die Auswahl,-en choice
Marmelade,-n jam

das Brötchen,- roll
Müsli cereal

nahrhaft nourishing
reichhaltig rich
zwischendurch in between

Cultural Note

An American-style breakfast is unusual in Germany, as it is almost everywhere in Europe. A standard German breakfast, **das Frühstück,** consists of rolls, butter and jam. In recent years hotels have made an effort to add to the variety on the breakfast table. Now you will often find **Aufschnitt** (a variety of sliced meats and sausages) and **Käse** (cheese) to eat with your **Brötchen** (roll). The demand for healthier foods also induced hotels to offer **Müsli** (cereal). Germans usually don't go out for breakfast and most restaurants (except hotels) don't offer it. Americans who expect to find a variety of egg dishes with ham and potatoes on the menu will be disappointed.

Sonja: Allerdings muß man nichts mehr zwischendurch essen, wenn man ein reichhaltiges Frühstück zu sich nimmt. Im Hotel Graef gibt es Fruchtsäfte — sehr gesund, Müsli —auch gesund, Aufschnitt — nichts für Vegetarier, Joghurt —sehr nahrhaft, Butter — macht dick, wenn man zuviel ißt, Früchte — mit vielen Vitaminen, und Brot. Natürlich gibt es zuhause nicht so eine fantastische Auswahl. Ich fragte: Was ißt du zum Frühstück?

E. **Alles klar? Machen Sie eine Liste: Was essen und trinken Sandra, Rina, Jan, Luca, Tina und Anna zum Frühstück** (for breakfast)?

Sandra: ____________________ ____________________ ____________________

Rina: ____________________ ____________________ ____________________

Jan: ____________________ ____________________ ____________________

Luca: ____________________ ____________________ ____________________

Tina: ____________________ ____________________ ____________________

Anna: ____________________ ____________________ ____________________

F. **FÜR ZWEI**

Was essen Sie zum Frühstück? Fragen Sie Ihre/n Partner/in, was sie oder er gern zum Frühstück ißt. Machen Sie eine Liste.

chapter 5 to 6

Scene 4: Eating Out

der Big Mac,-s
Cheeseburger,-

die Apfeltasche,-n apple fritter
Chips here: french fries

bestellen to order
trauen + dat. plural to trust

ausländisch foreign
griechisch Greek

bayrisch Bavarian
türkisch Turkish

am vollsten here: most crowded
das macht dick this is fattening
eine Fülle von an abundance of, a variety of
ist so that's how it is
nicht unbedingt not necessarily
Was wird am meisten verkauft? What do you sell the most?
zur Verfügung stehen to be available

Cultural Note

In traditional German custom the **Mittagessen** (lunch) is the big meal of the day. As work habits have changed a lot during the last 50 years, fewer people want to eat too much at lunch time. Consequently, more and more people now eat their big meal in the evening. A traditional German **Mittagessen** consists of soup, meat, potatoes or pasta, gravy and a salad.

Sonja: Wenn man mittags oder abends essen gehen möchte, stehen einem eine Fülle von Restaurants zur Verfügung. Man kann italienisch, griechisch, türkisch oder bayrisch essen gehen.

On Screen

Seit 1971 gibt es McDonald's in Deutschland. Pro Tag kommen 760.000 Gäste. Der Nettoumsatz beträgt mehr als eine Milliarde DM.
McDonald's restaurants have been in Germany since 1971. Every day they cater to 760,000 customers. They net more than 1 billion marks annually.

(At McDonald's)

Sonja: Was ißt du da?
Girl: Pommes Frites und 'ne Apfeltasche.
Sonja: Wie teuer war das?
Girl: 3,80.
Sonja: Macht das dick?
Girl: Die Pommes bestimmt und die Apfeltasche auch. Aber man ißt es ja nicht jeden Tag.

Sonja: Ißt du auch mal gerne ausländisch?
Girl: Ja, griechisch, italienisch, chinesisch.

Sonja: Ißt du auch mal ausländisch?
Man: Nie.
Sonja: Nie?
Man: Ich eß' nie ausländisch, weil man dem auch nicht trauen kann.

Sonja: Was ißt du gerade?
Girl: Mexicana-Salat.
Sonja: Wie teuer war der?
Girl: 4,15.
Sonja: Glaubst du, der ist gesund?
Girl: Vielleicht nicht unbedingt, aber er schmeckt.

Sonja: Was ißt du da?
Boy: Ja, einen Hamburger, Pommes und 'nen Kaffee.
Sonja: Was kostet das?
Boy: 6 Mark 50.
Sonja: Meinst du, das macht dick?
Boy: Ja, macht wohl dick, ja, aber was schmeckt, macht dick. Ist so.

Sonja: Was ißt du gerade?
Girl: Chicken McNuggets und Pommes Frites.
Sonja: Wie teuer war das?
Girl: 5 Mark 55.

Sonja: Macht das nicht dick?
Girl: Es gibt viele Dinge, die dick machen, aber — dies wird wohl auch dazugehören.

Sonja: Was ißt du da?
Boy: Einen Cheeseburger.
Sonja: Wieviel hat der gekostet?
Boy: 2 Mark 15.

Sonja: Was ißt du da?
Woman: Hamburger und Chips.
Sonja: Und wieviel hat das zusammen gekostet?
Woman: Ungefähr 7 Mark 10.
Sonja: Und schmeckt das?
Woman: Okay.

Sonja: Was wird am meisten verkauft?
Manager: Big Macs.
Sonja: Und wann ist es hier am vollsten?
Manager: Zwischen 12 Uhr und 14 Uhr.
Sonja: Was für Leute kommen hierher?
Manager: Leute, die kommen, sind meist Jugendliche oder Leute, die in Büros arbeiten und haben nur kurze Zeit zu essen.

G. **Alles klar?** Answer the following questions.

1. Seit wann gibt es McDonald's in Deutschland?

   ____

2. Was kostet DM 3, 80? ______________________________

   DM 4, 15? ______________________________

   DM 6, 50? ______________________________

   DM 5, 55? ______________________________

   DM 7, 10? ______________________________

   DM 2, 15? ______________________________

3. Welches Gericht ist sehr populär?______________________________

4. Um wieviel Uhr essen die meisten Leute bei McDonald's?______________________________

   ____

5. Was für Leute essen bei McDonald's?______________________________

6. Wie schmeckt den Deutschen das Essen bei McDonald's? ______________________________

   ____

7. Ist das Essen bei McDonald's gesund? ______________________________

8. Warum ist McDonald's so beliebt (popular) in Deutschland? Was glauben Sie? _______

   ____

H. **FÜR ZWEI**

Essen Sie auch bei McDonald's? Talk to your partner about your attitude toward fast food.

> ### *Grammar Note*
>
> Adjectival nouns following **etwas** (something) and **nichts** (nothing) take neuter primary endings and are capitalized.
>
> For example: Es gibt **nichts Italienisches** auf der Speisekarte. (nothing Italian)
> Ich bestelle **etwas Leichtes**. (something light)

I. **Was bestellen Sie, wenn...**

Beispiel: ...Sie gesund essen möchten? - Etwas Leichtes.

1. ...das Wetter kalt ist?
2. ...Sie krank sind?
3. ...Sie großen Hunger haben?
4. ...das Wetter sehr warm ist?
5. ...Sie wenig Geld haben?
6. ...Sie wenig Zeit haben?
7. ...Ihre/n Freund/in zum Abendessen einladen?

J. **FÜR EINE/N, ZWEI ODER MEHRERE -** PUZZLE

The letters in the shaded squares spell the name of a delicious ice cream dessert!

1. meal
2. to order
3. rich (food)
4. cereal
5. hot, spicy
6. strawberries
7. meat
8. diet
9. vegetarian
10. roll
11. delicious

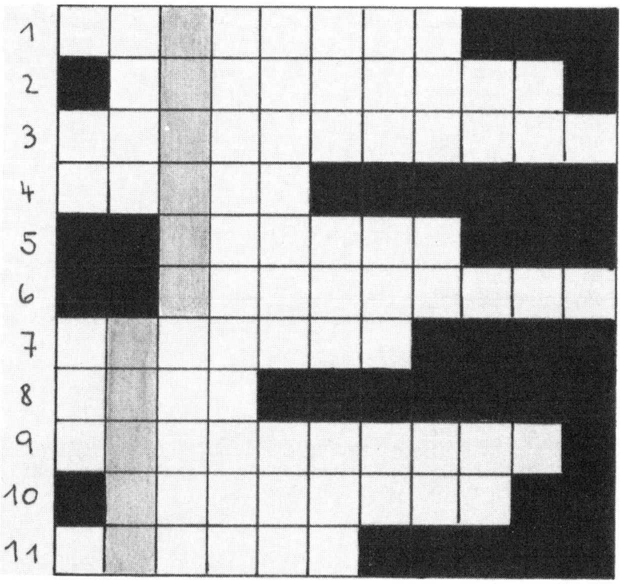

Scene 5: Eating Meat vs. Being a Vegetarian

der Vegetarier,- vegetarian (m.)
die Vegetarierin,-nen vegetarian (fem.)
das Fett,-e fat

vermissen to miss

allzuviel too much
dauernd all the time

bewußt conscious, aware

das wär' nichts für mich not for me, I wouldn't like that
gar nicht schlecht not so bad
hin und wieder every now and then
Könntest du dir vorstellen, Vegetarier zu werden? Could you imagine becoming a vegetarian?
überhaupt nicht not at all

On Screen

Diese jungen Männer möchten Köche werden. Sie bereiten gerade osso bucco vor. Osso bucco ist ein italienisches Gericht und besteht aus Kalbfleisch.
These young men would like to become cooks. Right now they are preparing osso bucco. Osso bucco is an Italian dish made from veal.

Sonja:	Die meisten Menschen essen heute viel bewußter als früher. Einige meiner Freunde essen kein Fleisch, sind Vegetarier. Ich fragte: Ißt du Fleisch?
Jan:	Nicht so gern. Ich bin schon seit 3 Jahren Vegetarier.
Sonja:	Vermißt du es manchmal?
Jan:	Nee, überhaupt nicht. Mir schmeckt das nicht.
Sonja:	Kannst du dir vorstellen, einmal Vegetarier zu werden?
Anna:	Nein, weil ich auch finde, daß Fleisch hin und wieder gar nicht schlecht ist.
Sonja:	Ißt du Fleisch?
Nicole:	Nicht sehr oft, aber eigentlich schon.
Sonja:	Könntest du dir vorstellen, einmal Vegetarier zu werden?
Nicole:	Ja, ich mach's manchmal 2 Wochen oder so, aber nicht immer, aber ich könnt's mir vorstellen.
Sonja:	Ißt du Fleisch?
Thomas:	Ja, aber nicht allzuviel, also ich versuche, wenig Fett zu essen.
Sonja:	Ißt du Fleisch?
Petra:	Nicht mehr soviel wie früher, vielleicht zweimal in der Woche.
Sonja:	Warum ißt du weniger Fleisch?
Petra:	Weil es nicht so gesund ist, und man sollte eben weniger Fleisch essen.
Sonja:	Kannst du dir vorstellen, einmal Vegetarier zu werden?
Miriam:	Eigentlich nicht so sehr, weil dauernd nur Gemüse und so, das wär' nichts für mich.

K. Alles klar? Check the appropriate answer for each person.

Wer ißt Fleisch?	**oft**	**manchmal**	**nie**
Jan:	________	________	________
Anna:	________	________	________
Nicole:	________	________	________
Thomas:	________	________	________
Petra:	________	________	________
Miriam:	________	________	________

Warum essen immer mehr Leute kein Fleisch?

L. **FÜR ZWEI**

Könnten Sie sich vorstellen, Vegetarier zu werden? Discuss your eating habits with your partner.

Beispiel: Ich könnte mir nicht vorstellen,

Ich	**könnte mir (nicht) vorstellen....**			
	versuche....			
		mehr	**Gemüse**	
		weniger	**Fleisch**	**zu essen.**
		kein,-	**Obst**	
			Bier	
			Süßigkeiten	
			Hamburger	**zu trinken.**
			Kaffee	
			Salat	

Scene 6: What People Drink

chapter 7 to 8

der Hopfen hops
Liter,- liter

die Bierbrauerei,-en brewery
Diät,-en diet
Gerste barley
Limo,-s = Limonade,-n lemonade, soft drink

das Radler half beer and half lemonade

dürr skinny
gemütlich cozy, comfy, informal
schädlich unhealthy, bad

eine Diät machen to be on a diet
Ich kann es mir leisten. I can afford it.
Schmeckt's? Does it taste good?

Ein Biergarten

Cultural Note

As most people know, Germany has a longstanding tradition of brewing beer. Every region prides itself on its own local brew and beer-drinking customs. Almost every German restaurant or pub has a **Stammtisch**, a table reserved for regular customers who go there to meet friends, drink beer, play cards, and discuss politics.

On Screen

In München gibt es 7 Bierbrauereien, die 510 Millionen Liter Bier im Jahr produzieren. Bier darf nur aus natürlichen Produkten hergestellt werden: Wasser, Hopfen und Gerste.

There are 7 breweries in Munich which produce 510 million liters of beer annually. Beer must be made of natural ingredients such as water, hops, and barley.

Sonja: Wenn man eine Diät macht, sollte man auch keinen Alkohol trinken. Aber hier in München trinkt fast jeder Bier. Und außerdem sind die Biergärten sehr schön und gemütlich.

Sonja: Was trinkst du da?
Young woman 1: Das ist Bier und Limo (Radler).
Sonja: Schmeckt das gut?
Young woman 1: Ja.
Sonja: Aber es ist mit Alkohol?
Young woman 1: Ja.
Sonja: Macht das nicht dick?
Young woman 1: Na ja, kann schon sein, ja schon, also wenn man zuviel trinkt, sicher.

M. <u>Alles klar</u>? Answer the following questions.

1. Wie viele Bierbrauereien gibt es in München?

   ____

2. Wo kann man in München Bier trinken?

   ____

3. Warum sollte man kein Bier trinken, wenn man eine Diät macht?

____

4. Was ist ein Radler?

____

5. Was kostet ein Radler?

____

6. Warum ist ein Radler nicht so schädlich wie Bier?

____

Cultural Note

Germany is not only known for its famous beers but also for a longstanding tradition of making wine. Nearly two thousand years ago winegrowing was introduced by the Romans and has since been successfully practiced in the river valleys of Western and Southern Germany where the climate is moderate. The winegrowing villages along the **Mosel, Rhein, Main,** and **Neckar** valleys have their annual **Weinfest** organized by local residents who celebrate the harvest of their new wine. Some of the grapes grown in Germany are **Riesling, Müller-Thurgau, Silvaner, Trollinger, and Spätburgunder.**

chapter 8 to 9

Scene 7: Asking About Diets

das Gewicht weight
Mineralwasser mineral water
Übergewicht excess weight

ab/nehmen (nimmt ab) to lose weight
auf/passen (paßt auf) to pay attention
zu/nehmen (nimmt zu) to gain weight

etwas nötig haben to need something
im Gegenteil on the contrary
Übergewicht haben to be overweight

Sonja:	Es stimmt leider. Die leckersten Dinge im Leben machen dick, und wenn man nicht aufpaßt, hat man leicht Übergewicht. Ich fragte: Machst du manchmal eine Diät?
Rina:	Ja, manchmal.
Sonja:	Was ißt du dann?
Rina:	Obst, und ich trink' viel Mineralwasser.
Sonja:	Machst du eine Diät?
Sandra:	Diät? Nee, nein, hab' ich das nötig?
Niklas:	Nein, die hab' ich nicht nötig.
Albrecht:	Ich mach' keine Diät. Mit Nahrung hab' ich überhaupt keine Probleme. Im Gegenteil: Ich nehm' viel zu schnell ab.
Sonja:	Machst du eine Diät?
Peter:	Ja.
Sonja:	Und was für eine?
Peter:	FDH. Friß die Hälfte.
Sonja:	Machst du eine Diät?
Shamin:	Ja.
Sonja:	Was für eine?
Shamin:	Wasser, Tees und Säfte.
Sonja:	Machen Sie irgendeine Diät?
Helmut Lang:	Nein.

N. FÜR ZWEI

You are a dietician and have to come up with a dietary plan for one week including daily breakfast, lunch and dinner. Discuss the plan with your partner.

PROGRAMM 16

KLEIDER MACHEN LEUTE

This episode deals with clothing and fashion. Sonja interviews a number of teens in order to find out what they wear and how much money they spend on clothing. We visit a fashion show in Munich and learn what kind of clothes some of the professional models wear. Finally Sonja shows us some bargains at a flea market.

Mode im Schaufenster

LANGUAGE FUNCTIONS

- describing clothing
- going shopping
- stating opinions

CONTENTS

- fashion and prices
- what Germans wear
- superlative
- relative clauses
- adjective endings

chapter 9 to 15

Scene 1: How Much Do Teens Spend on Clothes?

chapter 10 to 11

die Designermode,- designer fashions
Klamotten (plural) coll. for clothes

das Sweatshirt,-s
T-Shirt,-s

aus/geben (gibt aus) to spend
aus/kommen (kommt aus) to make do, to cope
differieren to vary
schätzen to guess, presume
sich etwas leisten to afford something

chic = schick elegant, fancy
modisch fashionable
ungefähr approximately

Sonja: Designermode ist chic, wenn man sie sich leisten kann. Aber wenn man noch zur Schule geht, geht das nicht, und vielleicht hättest du auch gar keine Lust, Designerklamotten zu tragen. Jetzt wollen wir einmal sehen, was Jugendliche tragen — in der Schule, der Freizeit oder zur Arbeit. Ich fragte zuerst: Wieviel Geld gibst du im Monat für Kleidung aus?

Magnus: 250 Mark.
Sonja: Und was für Sachen kaufst du?
Magnus: Hauptsächlich Jeans, Sweatshirts, T-Shirts.

Sonja: Wieviel Geld gibst du ungefähr im Monat für Kleidung aus?
Niklas: Ungefähr 200 Mark.
Sonja: Was für Kleidung kaufst du?
Niklas: Ja, Schuhe, Sweatshirts, Hosen — das differiert ein bißchen.

A. Alles klar? Make a list of what the interviewed people wear and how much they spend on clothes every month.

	Wieviel geben sie für Kleidung aus?	Was für Sachen kaufen sie?
Magnus:	*DM 250*	*Jeans, Sweatshirts, T-Shirts*
Niklas:		
Sandra:		
Luca:		
Heike:		

Jan: ____________________

Vanessa: ____________________ ____

Nicole: ____________________ ____

B. **FÜR ZWEI**

Discuss your monthly expenses with your partner.

Remember: Adjectival nouns following **etwas** (something) and **nichts** (nothing) take neuter endings.

Beispiel:

Ich kaufe mir sportliche Kleidung.
Ich kaufe mir **etwas Sportliches.** (something sporty)

Aber:

Sometimes people say **was** instead of **etwas**:
was Schickes (something fancy)
or they omit the **etwas** altogether:
Sportliches (sporty things)

C. **Was tragen Sie, wenn...**

1. ...Sie in die Oper gehen?

2. ...das Wetter kalt ist?

3. ...Sie Tennis spielen wollen?

4. ...Sie ins Kino gehen?

5. ...das Wetter sehr warm ist?

6. ...Sie zur Uni gehen?

7. ...Sie Ihr Auto waschen oder reparieren?

8. ...Ihre/n Freund/in zum Abendessen einladen?

Grammar Note

Remember the adjective endings with a preceding ein-word.

	ein Pulli	eine Hose	ein Sweatshirt	meine Schuhe
Nom.	roter	(e) kurze	altes	neuen
Acc.	(en) roten	(e) kurze	altes	neuen
Dat.	(em) roten	(er) kurzen	(em) alten	(n) neuen
Gen.	(es) roten	(er) kurzen	(es) alten	(r) neuen

Beispiel: Das ist ein rote**r** Pulli. **oder:** Ich kaufe eine**n** rote**n** Pulli.
oder: Seine neue**n** Schuhe haben DM 500 gekostet.
Mit deinem kurze**n** Rock kannst du nicht in die Oper gehen!

D. **Übung:** Rewrite using the correct adjective ending.

Beispiel: Hier ist eine Hose, die **modisch** ist.
Hier ist eine modische Hose.

Sie trägt einen Pulli, der **gelb** ist.
Sie trägt einen gelben Pulli.

1. Ich kaufe einen Anzug, der **teuer** ist.
2. Sie hat ein Kleid, das **sportlich** ist.
3. Sie arbeitet mit Klamotten, die **alt** sind.
4. Jeans, die **schwarz** sind, gefallen ihm nicht.
5. Er möchte einen Mantel, der **lang** ist.
6. Wir können uns nur Klamotten leisten, die **billig** sind.

Scene 2: The Most Expensive Item

chapter 11 to 12

das **Jackett,-s** jacket
Sakko,-s jacket

die **Jeansjacke,-n** jeans jacket
Lederjacke,-n leather jacket

an/probieren (probiert an) to try on

Das steht Ihnen (gut)! That suits you (well)!

> *On Screen*
>
> **Die bekanntesten Warenhäuser in Deutschland sind Karstadt, Kaufhof, Horten und C&A.**
> The most popular department stores in Germany are Karstadt, Kaufhof, Horten and C&A.

Jan: Ja, die ist doch wunderbar.
Luca: Die ist schön. Aber ich probier' erst mal die andere an.
Jan: Die Farbe ist schöner.
Luca: Oh nee, die ist zu klein.
Jan: Gut, nehmen wir die andere.

Luca: Ich nehm' die Jacke hier.
Clerk: Ja — 359, bitte.

Sonja: Hast du dir die Jacke gekauft?
Luca: Ja, die hab' ich mir gekauft.
Sonja: Wie teuer war sie?
Luca: 359 DM.
Sonja: Ist das das Teuerste, was du dir je gekauft hast?
Luca: Nein, ich hab' mir schon mal ein Kaschmirsakko für ungefähr 600 DM gekauft.

E. <u>Alles klar</u>?

1. Was für Kleidungsstücke probiert Luca an?

2. Was hat die Jacke gekostet, die er sich gekauft hat?

3. Hat Luca sich schon einmal etwas Teures gekauft? Was war das, und was hat es gekostet?

F. Watch scene 2 and complete the list below.

	Was war ihr teuerstes Kleidungsstück und	**was hat es gekostet?**
Rina	______________________	____________
Boris	______________________	____________
Alexander	______________________	____________
Nicole	______________________	____________
Miriam	______________________	____________
Bernd	______________________	____________
Petra	______________________	____________

G. **FÜR ZWEI.**

Was tragen Sie (nicht) gern? Wo kaufen Sie die Kleidung?
Describe which clothes you like. Use adjectives to describe the things you like. Talk to your partner about your preferences.

Beispiel: Elegante Kleidung gefällt mir.
Ich finde italienische Kleidung attraktiv.

lang-			
warm-			
kurz-	**Hemden**		
alt-	**Jacken**		
hell-	**Mäntel**	**finde ich**	**hübsch**
modisch-	**Blusen**		**langweilig**
elegant-	**Röcke**		
bequem-	**Anzüge**		
eng-	**Jeans**	**gefallen mir (nicht)**	
dunkel-	**Kleidung**	**gefällt**	
exotisch-	**Kleider**		
schwarz-	**Hosen**	**stehen mir (nicht)** (suit me)	
italienisch-	**Hüte**	**steht mir (nicht)**	
sportlich-	**Kostüme**		
praktisch-			
?	**?**		

H. **FÜR ZWEI: Modemagazin**

Take a fashion magazine to class. Describe the clothes of one of the models to your partner/s who will make a drawing from what you say. Discuss the results, then change roles.

Scene 3: A Visit to a Fashion Show

der **Käufer,-** buyer
Modedesigner,- fashion designer
Visagist,-en make-up artist
Zufall,-"e contingency, chance

die **Filmrolle,-n** part in a film
Modewoche,-n week-long fashion exhibit of the latest designs

das **Design,-s** design
Fotomodell,-e model
Indonesien Indonesia
Model,-s fashion model
Modezentrum,-zentren fashion center
Paar,-e pair
Praktikum pl. **Praktika** practical training
Zentrum pl. **Zentren** center

Modenschau

entdecken to discover

je = jemals ever
lässig casual
zeitlos classic
klassisch classic
namhaft well-known, famous

aus aller Welt from all over the world
aus Zufall by chance
es hat sich so ergeben it turned out that way
...wurde mal angesprochen I was once asked

Adjective endings preceded by a <u>der</u>-word

	der Mantel	die Hose	das Kleidungsstück	die Schuhe
Nom.	längste	schönste	schmutzige	teuersten
Acc.	den längsten	schönste	schmutzige	teuersten
Dat.	dem längsten	der schönsten	dem schmutzigen	den teuersten
Gen.	des längsten	der schönsten	des schmutzigen	der teuersten

Indem is a conjunction and is generally translated as "by". For example:

Man wird Visagist, <u>indem</u> man ein Praktikum <u>macht</u>.
You become a make-up artist by undergoing practical training.

Sonja: München ist—genau wie London, Rom oder Paris—ein internationales Modezentrum. Jedes Jahr findet hier die Modewoche statt. Käufer aus aller Welt kommen, um die neuesten Designs zu sehen.

On Screen

Auf der Modewoche präsentieren 802 Aussteller aus 8 Ländern rund 3000 Kollektionen für Herbst und Winter.
During the annual fashion week 802 exhibitors from eight different countries present approximately 3,000 collections for fall and winter.

Sonja: Wie heißt du?
Peter: Peter.
Sonja: Und wie alt bist du?
Peter: 21 Jahre.
Sonja: Was ist dein Beruf?
Peter: Visagist.
Sonja: Wie wird man Visagist?
Peter: Visagist wird man ganz einfach, indem man 'n Praktikum macht bei'm namhaften Visagisten.

Sonja: Wie heißt du?
Shamin: Shamin.
Sonja: Wie alt bist du?
Shamin: 26.
Sonja: Was bist du von Beruf?
Shamin: Model.
Sonja: Model. Und wie bist du Model geworden?
Shamin: Eigentlich mehr so aus Zufall — wurde mal angesprochen und hat sich so ergeben.
Sonja: Wieviel Geld gibst du im Monat für Kleidung aus?
Shamin: 500 bis 1000 Mark.
Sonja: Und was kaufst du dir?
Shamin: Klassische, zeitlose, moderne Sachen.
Sonja: Kannst du dich erinnern, was das teuerste Kleidungsstück war, das du je gekauft hast?
Shamin: Ca. 1000 Mark.
Sonja: Und was war's?
Shamin: Das war'n Kaschmirmantel.

I. <u>Alles klar</u>?

1. Warum kommen Käufer aus aller Welt zur Modewoche nach München?
2. Was machen die Aussteller auf der Modewoche?
3. Wie alt ist Peter?
4. Wie ist Peter Visagist geworden?
5. Wie alt ist Shamin?
6. Wie ist Shamin Model geworden?
7. Wieviel Geld gibt Shamin jeden Monat für Kleidung aus?
8. Was war das teuerste Kleidungsstück, das sie sich je gekauft hat?

J. **FÜR ZWEI: Personal shopper**

Imagine one of you is a busy executive who lacks time to shop for his/her own clothes. The other one is his/her personal shopper who has very clear ideas about what the person should wear. Talk about the various occasions for which new clothes are needed. Make suggestions about what the clothes should look like and discuss them. (You might not always agree!)

Cultural Note

Germans are very fashion conscious and often pay a lot of attention to what people wear. If you go to expensive restaurants or hotels, you will have to be dressed appropriately. It is uncommon to wear sweatpants or sportswear around town or to the grocery store. However, corporate America seems more conservative with regard to its dress code than corporate Germany. German business executives have a larger selection of styles to choose from.

Grammar

Relative clauses are introduced by relative pronouns (that, which, who, whose, whom). The German relative pronouns are identical to the definite articles, except for the dative plural (denen) and the genitive forms (dessen, deren, dessen, deren).

The relative pronoun refers to a certain word (or phrase) in the preceding main clause. For example:

> Das war **das** teuerste Kleidungsstück, **das** ich mir je gekauft habe.
> This was the most expensive piece of clothing (that) I ever bought.
> **Aber:** Das war der teuerste Mantel, **den** ich mir je gekauft habe.

Since **der teuerste Mantel** functions as the direct object of the verb in the relative clause, the relative pronoun is in the accusative form.

K. **Übung.** Fill in the blanks using the appropriate relative pronouns and adjective endings.

1. Was hat der teuer____ Kaschmirmantel gekostet, ______________ sich Shamin gekauft hat?
2. Das ist der heißest____ Sommer, ______________ ich je erlebt habe.
3. Können Sie sich an die rot____ Jacke erinnern, ______________ ich meiner Mutter geschenkt habe?
4. München ist die schönst____ Stadt, in ______________ ich je gelebt habe.
5. Hendra ist der indonesisch____ Modedesigner, ______________ seine eigene Kleidung trägt.
6. Wie heißt die deutsch____ Stadt, in ______________ jedes Jahr eine Modewoche stattfindet?
7. Was hat der dunkl____ Anzug gekostet, mit ______________ Boris in die Oper gehen will?
8. Wie heißt die jung____ Frau, ______________ Kaschmirmantel 1000 Mark gekostet hat?

L. **FÜR ZWEI ODER GRUPPEN**

Define the following words using a relative clause.

Model: **Viktualienmarkt: Ein Markt, auf dem man Obst und Gemüse kaufen kann.**
Kaschmirmantel: Ein Mantel, der aus Kaschmir ist.

1. Stadtkleidung
2. Designermode
3. Lederjacke
4. Sonnenhut
5. Warenhaus
6. Bermudahose
7. Wintermantel
8. Fotomodell
9. Schaufenster
10. Spazierstock
11. Skianzug
12. Faschingskostüm
13. Flohmarkt

M. **Watch and listen!** Have your pencil ready and make a list!

	Was ist das teuerste Kleidungsstück, das sie sich je gekauft haben?	Was hat es gekostet?
Shamin:	______________________	______________
Hendra Ramli:	______________________	______________
Albrecht:	______________________	______________

	Wieviel geben sie im Monat für Kleidung aus?
Sebastian:	______________________
P. C. Hall:	______________________

N. **FÜR ZWEI**

Können Sie sich erinnern, was das teuerste Kleidungsstück war, das Sie sich je gekauft haben? Talk to your partner using the model below.

Beispiel: Der teuerste Pullover, **den** ich mir je gekauft habe, hat $100 gekostet.

Der teuerste Pullover,		
Die schönste Jacke,	die	
Die beste Hose,		
Das letzte Hemd,	das	ich mir je gekauft habe, hat $... gekostet.
Die teuersten Schuhe,		
Der teuerste Anzug,	den	
Das billigste Kleid,		
?		

Und wieviel geben Sie jeden Monat für Kleidung aus? Talk to your partner about how much you spend on clothing.

O. **FÜR GRUPPEN: Berühmte Schauspieler in bekannten Rollen**

One of you thinks of a movie star in a well-known film. Describe what he/she was wearing. The others have to guess the film and who the star is. Describe a characteristic scene if necessary. (Use past tense!)

Scene 4: What Is in Style and What to Wear to School

chapter 13 to 14

der Geschmack taste, liking
Rapper,- rap (group) wear
Unterschied,-e difference

die Kapuze,-n hood
Schuluniform,-en school uniform

an/haben (hat an) to wear
an/ziehen (zieht an) to put on; to wear
was = etwas
ist angezogen is dressed, wears

(das ist) verschieden it varies, it depends
auf jeden Fall anyway, in any case, anyhow
aus den 60er Jahren from the sixties
breit wide
einheitlich here: the same
gerade now
hättest du gern...? would you like?
ich bin nicht sicher I'm not sure
in eine Uniform reingepreßt crammed into a uniform
mal sehen let's see
momentan these days, at the moment
normalerweise normally, usually
unpraktisch impractical, inconvenient, unsuitable
wie's dem Geschmack entspricht to one's taste/liking
ziemlich rather

Sonja: Ich bin nicht sicher, ob mir diese supermodischen Sachen überhaupt stehen würden. Auf jeden Fall wären sie für die Schule ziemlich unpraktisch. Mal sehen, was Münchner Jugendliche wirklich tragen.
I am not sure, whether these fancy things would suit me at all. They would be rather unsuitable for school, anyway. Let's see what Munich teens really wear.

Sonja: Ziehst du an, was modern ist oder was dir gefällt?
Jan: Nee, was mir gefällt. Ich mag gern Sachen, so Sachen aus den 60er Jahren, so.

Nicole: Verschieden. Meistens gefällt mir das, was gerade modern ist.
Sonja: Was ist gerade modern?
Nicole: Bei uns eher so Flower-Power, so 70er Jahre.

Sonja: Was ist momentan in?
Miriam: Ja die breiten Hosen und die Turnschuhe und T-Shirts oder, nee, Sweatshirts mit Kapuze hinten, also so Rapper halt.
Sonja: Was ziehst du normalerweise zur Schule an?
Miriam: Genauso wie ich jetzt was anhab', also ist kein Unterschied.
Sonja: Gibt's bei euch eine Schuluniform?
Miriam: Das gibt's bei uns nicht in Deutschland.
Sonja: Hättest du gern eine Uniform?
Miriam: Nee, nein.
Sonja: Warum nicht?
Miriam: Ja, weil dann jeder so einheitlich angezogen ist, und schön sind sie meistens auch nicht.

Sonja: Hättest du gern eine Schuluniform?
Petra: Nein, möchte ich nicht.
Sonja: Warum nicht?
Petra: Weil ich finde, man sollte sich so anziehen, wie's einem gefällt und nicht wie das die Schule sagt.
Sonja: Würdest du gern eine Schuluniform haben?
Tina: Nein, würd' ich nicht.
Sonja: Warum nicht?

Tina: Weil ich find', jeder soll sich so anziehen wie's seinem Geschmack entspricht und nicht in irgend 'ne Uniform reingepreßt werden.

Sonja: Was ziehst du normalerweise zur Schule an?
Thomas: So wie ich jetzt rumlaufe.

Luca: Zur Schule ziehe ich eigentlich dasselbe an, was ich sonst in meiner Freizeit auch anziehe.

P. Alles klar?

1. **Was tragen Münchner Jugendliche wirklich? Machen Sie eine Liste!**

   Jan: ______________________________

   ____

   Nicole: ______________________________

   ____

   Miriam: ______________________________

   ____

2. **Was ziehen deutsche Jugendliche zur Schule an?**

3. **Warum wollen Miriam, Petra und Tina keine Uniform tragen?**

Q. **FÜR ZWEI**

Finden Sie, man sollte eine Uniform tragen? Discuss the issue with your partner using the model below.

Beispiel: Ich glaube, man sollte sich so anziehen, wie's einem gefällt.

Ich	**meine,** **finde,** **glaube,**	**man sollte (sich)...**	
		in die Oper	**eine Uniform tragen**
		als Kellner	**so anziehen, wie in der Freizeit**
		als Krankenschwester	**so anziehen, wie's einem gefällt**
		zu Hause	**schön anziehen**
		zur Uni	**lässige Kleidung tragen**
		zur Schule	**kurze Hosen tragen**
		ins Büro	**einen Minirock tragen**

chapter 14 to 15

Scene 5: Shopping at a Flea Market

der Flohmarkt,¨-e flea market
Laden,¨- store
Kerzenhalter,- candlestick
Ring,-e ring

die Platte,-n = Schallplatte,-n record
Kerze,-n candle

ausgefallen peculiar, exceptional
egal all the same
günstig reasonably priced
jedenfalls anyway
originell original, unusual
witzig funny
zufrieden content

ab und zu now and then
ein guter Kauf a good buy, bargain
zum Schluß finally, in the end

On Screen

Flohmärkte finden fast immer am Wochenende statt, im Sommer auch oft draußen. Man kann alles mögliche günstig ersteigern: Kleider, Bücher, Schallplatten, Krims Krams.

Flea markets almost always take place on the weekend—in summer often outside. You can get bargains on all kinds of things: clothes, books, records, and other odds and ends.

R. **Fill in the blanks as you watch video scene 5.**

Sonja: Möchte man nicht zu viel Geld für ______________ ausgeben, kann man auf den Flohmarkt gehen und second-hand-Kleidung ______________ . Es gibt dort oft billige und originelle Sachen. Original bayrisch!
If one does not want to spend too much on clothes, one can go to the flea market and buy second-hand clothes. There are cheap and unusual things. Genuinely Bavarian!

Woman: Jetzt zum Schluß jedes Stück 3 Mark. Ob Hose, Rock, egal—alles 3 Mark.

Sonja: Wieviel hat das gekostet?

Woman 2: Darf ich das sagen? ______________ .

Sonja: Und sind Sie damit zufrieden?

Woman 2: Das war'n guter ______________ jedenfalls.

Sonja: Warum gehst du zum Flohmarkt?

Sandra: Weil's hier witzige, ausgefallene ______________ gibt.

Sonja: Und wonach suchst du?

Sandra: Nach, nach Mode, die's einfach in ______________ nicht mehr zu kaufen gibt, nach originellen Sachen.

Sonja: Und wonach suchst du?

Werner: Ach, ich such' ab und zu nach ______________ , die's nicht mehr gibt in den Läden — da findet man gute Sachen.

Sonja: Warum gehst du zum Flohmarkt?

Christine: Ja, um in ______________ Sachen rumzukramen, weil man oft billige Sachen findet, die gut sind...

Sonja: Und wonach suchst du?

Christine: Ja, nach Kleidung und nach Platten und ______________ .

Sonja: Seht mal, was ich mir gekauft hab' - einen Kerzenhalter für ______________ und einen Ring für 50.

S. <u>Alles klar</u>?

1. Wann finden Flohmärkte statt?

2. Was kann man auf Flohmärkten kaufen?

3. Warum gehen die Leute auf den Flohmarkt?

Jan: ______________________________

Vanessa: ______________________________

Nicole: ______________________________

T. **FÜR ZWEI ODER GRUPPEN: Vorher, nachher**

Do you agree with the pictures or should **vorher** be **nachher** and **nachher** be **vorher**? Under which circumstances would **vorher** be **nachher**? Discuss your opinion with your partner(s).

PROGRAMM 17

WAS MÖCHTEST DU SPÄTER WERDEN?

Sonja asks several teenagers about their plans concerning their professional future. We learn about the German educational system and meet students of several professional training schools **(Berufsschulen)** for cooks, beer brewers, auto mechanics, dental technicians, and fashion designers.

Sonja auf dem Flohmarkt

LANGUAGE FUNCTIONS

- talking about future plans
- inquiring about careers
- providing reasons
- stating want / desire

CONTENTS

- the German school system
- professional training
- passive voice

chapter 1 to 7

Scene 1: What Would You Like to Be?

chapter 2 to 3

der Arzt,¨-e physician
Astronaut,-en astronaut
Bäcker,- baker
Bauer,-n farmer
Gesangsunterricht singing lessons
Geschäftsmann,¨-er businessman
Kapitän,-e captain
Mensch,-en human being; pl. people
Pilot,-en pilot
Rechtsanwalt,¨-e lawyer
Schauspieler,- actor
Tänzer,- dancer
Umgang interaction
Verkäufer,- salesman

die Ärztin,-nen physician
Astronautin,-nen astronaut
Ausbildung,-en education, professional training
Bäuerin,-nen farmer
Designerin,-nen designer
Friseuse,-n hair dresser
Medizin medicine
Möglichkeit,-en possibility
Pilotin,-nen pilot
Raumfahrt space travel
Rechtsanwältin,-nen lawyer
Sängerin,-nen singer
Schauspielerin,-nen actress
Schauspielschule,-n acting school
Sendung,-en TV program
Sportmedizin sports medicine
Tänzerin,-nen dancer
Verkäuferin,-nen saleswoman
Zukunft future

das Jurastudium education for lawyers
Recht justice
Studium, Studien course of studies

auf/wachsen (wächst auf) to grow up
dauern to last

denken an to think about
moderieren to moderate
sich etwas überlegen to think about something
unzählig countless
zunächst first

Man kann dem Menschen zu seinem Recht verhelfen You can help people obtain justice.
Was möchtest du werden? What would you like to be/become?
Wie sieht das bei anderen aus? How about other people?
der Umgang mit Menschen interacting with people
ich hab' überhaupt noch keine Ahnung I don't have the faintest idea yet
sich den Arbeitstag selber einteilen to freely arrange one's working hours
Was interessiert dich daran? What aspect do you find particularly interesting?

Sonja: Wahrscheinlich werdet ihr bald anfangen, an eure Zukunft zu denken, an das, was ihr später einmal werden möchtet. Es gibt unzählige Möglichkeiten. Probably you will soon begin to think about your future, about what you would like to be later.

Ich möchte auf jeden Fall Schauspielerin werden. Es macht mir viel Spaß, diese Sendung zu moderieren. Ich möchte noch öfter fürs Theater und Fernsehen arbeiten. Aber zunächst muß ich vier Jahre auf die Schauspielschule. Doch wie sieht das bei anderen aus? Ich fragte: Was möchtest du später werden?
I definitely want to become an actress. Presenting this program is a lot of fun. Later I want to work for theater and television more often. But first I will have to go to acting school for four years. But how about other people? I asked: "What do you want to be?"

Monika: Rechtsanwalt.
Sonja: Und warum?
Monika: Weil man dadurch dem Menschen zu seinem Recht verhelfen kann, und mir macht der Umgang mit Menschen Spaß.
Sonja: Was für eine Ausbildung braucht man, um Rechtsanwalt zu werden?
Monika: Ein Jurastudium und das dauert so ca. sieben Jahre.

Sonja: Was möchtest du später werden?
Nicole: Ich möchte Sportmedizin studieren.
Sonja: Und warum?
Nicole: Ich mache sehr gerne Sport, und Medizin ist bei uns in der Familie. Meine Mutter ist Ärztin.
Sonja: Was möchtest du später werden?
Jan: Ich hab' überhaupt noch keine Ahnung, was ich später werden will, hab' mir noch nichts überlegt.

Verena: Ich weiß nicht genau. Ich möchte gern Bücher schreiben.
Marco: Ich möchte eigentlich Geschäftsmann werden.
Sonja: Was interessiert dich besonders daran?
Marco: Also da ist man halt unabhängig, kann machen was man will, kann sich seinen Arbeitstag selber einteilen.

Sonja: Was möchtest du später werden?
Anna: Ich möchte klassische Sängerin werden.
Sonja: Warum?
Anna: Weil ich die klassische Musik sehr gerne mag, weil ich damit aufgewachsen bin und weil ich auch sehr gern singe und Gesangsunterricht habe.

Sonja: Was möchtest du später werden?
Tina: Ich möchte Designerin werden.

Thomas: Ingenieur oder irgendwas in technischer Richtung.
Sonja: Was interessiert dich besonders daran?
Thomas: Also Raumfahrt oder so würd' mich interessieren —etwas für die Zukunft.

A. **Alles klar**? Make a list! **Was möchten sie werden?** Write down the individual career choices of the people interviewed.

Monika: ______________________ **Nicole:** ______________________

Jan: ______________________ **Verena:** ______________________

Marco: ______________________ **Anna:** ______________________

Tina: ______________________ **Thomas:** ______________________

B. **FÜR GRUPPEN: Beruferaten**

Imagine you are on the TV show **Beruferaten**. You need a panel and candidates whose professions have to be guessed.

RULES:

1. The candidates can make up professions, but try to use mostly those mentioned in the program.

2. Answers allowed are "yes" or "no", but "**nicht nur**" or "**auch**" may be accepted.

3. Each member of the panel may ask until he/she gets "no" for an answer or runs out of questions.

4. To start the questioning the candidate pantomimes, imitating what she/he does at work.

5. You can also choose a referee who knows the candidate's profession and with whom, in case of doubt, the candidate can discuss the answer.

Hints for questions:

- Do you produce or distribute something?
- Do you sell something?
- Do you work with others or alone?
- Do you work outside or inside?
- Could I need your service or the things you produce or sell?
- Do people come to you?
- Do you go to people?
- Do you help people?
- Can one eat what you produce?

Grammar

Remember: in subordinate clauses the verb is always in final position!

Sonja möchte Schauspielerin werden. Sie möchte noch öfter fürs Fernsehen arbeiten.
Sonja möchte Schauspielerin werden, weil sie gern noch öfter fürs Fernsehen arbeiten möchte.

In spoken German, people don't always obey this rule, but in writing it has to be obeyed.

C. **Und warum?** After watching the video for a second time, state the reasons people give for their professional choices. Use a subordinate clause with **weil**. (The video script will help you find the correct answer.)

For example:

Thomas: Ich möchte Ingenieur werden. Also Raumfahrt oder so würd' mich interessieren.
Thomas: Thomas möchte Ingenieur werden, weil ihn Raumfahrt interessiert.

Sonja: Sonja möchte Schauspielerin werden, **weil** ______________________

____

Monika: ______________________

____

Nicole: ______________________

____

Jan: ____

____

Marco: ____

____

Anna: ____

____

Thomas: ____

____

"Was möchtest du später werden?"

D. **FÜR ZWEI**

Was möchten Sie später werden? Talk to your partner about your vocational plans. Create your own sentences according to the model below.

Beispiel: **Ich möchte Arzt werden, weil man viel Geld verdienen kann.**
Ich möchte Automechaniker werden, weil Autos mich interessieren.

Ich möchte ____________________ werden, weil (man)...
(profession)

Biologie		
Technik	mich interessieren.	
der Umgang mit Menschen	mich interessiert.	
viel Geld	Spaß macht.	
Menschen		
Literatur	verdienen	
Musik	helfen	kann.
Reisen	haben	
Autos	hören	
Kunst		
viel Freizeit	?	
?		

Scene 2: Interviews at a Hotel School and a Brewery

chapter 3 to 4

der **Beruf,-e** profession, vocation
Brauer,- brewer
Gast,¨-e customer, guest
Kontakt,-e contact
Schulabschluß,¨-sse here: education
Vorgang,¨-e process, here: reaction
Zweig,-e branch

die **Anstellung,-en = Stelle,-n** job, position
Arbeitszeit,-en hours at work
Berufsschule,-n vocational school
Freizeit,-en free time, time off
Lehre,-n apprenticeship
Mittlere Reife high school diploma after 10th grade
Naturwissenschaft,-en natural science
Restaurantfachfrau,-en restaurant manager

aus/bilden (bildet aus; ausgebildet) to educate
stören to bother, disturb

anschließend afterwards
chemisch chemical
selbständig self employed
gastronomisch gastronomic
physikalisch physical
auf die Hand net income after taxes
knappe DM 2000 barely 2000 DM
mit Leuten in Kontakt kommen to be in touch with people
Was interessiert dich an dem Beruf? What is it that interests you in this profession?
Was reizt dich an dem Beruf? What is it that appeals to you in this profession?

Cultural Note

When a German student is in the fourth grade, parents and teachers decide about his or her educational future, based on tests and grades. Students continue their education in either the **Hauptschule, Realschule,** or the **Gymnasium.**

- The **Hauptschule** (grades 5-10) is for students who will later choose a blue collar profession.
- The **Realschule** (grades 5-10) is for those students who will often choose white collar professions, but who do not intend to study at a university. At the end of their education, these students have to pass an exam which is called **die mittlere Reife.**
- The **Gymnasium** (grades 5-13) is for students who hope to attend a university after passing a comprehensive exam called **das Abitur.**

Even those who go to a **Hauptschule** or **Realschule** are required to go to a vocational school while completing an apprenticeship. Because German students have very different educational backgrounds, Sonja asks in the following scene: "**Welchen Schulabschluß hast du?**" (What kind of a school diploma do you have?)

Sonja: An dieser Schule werden die Schüler zu gastronomischen Berufen ausgebildet. Die Ausbildung dauert 3 Jahre und anschließend können sie in Hotels oder Restaurants arbeiten.

Sonja: Was für einen Schulabschluß hast du?
Antonio: Ich hab' die Mittlere Reife gemacht.
Sonja: Und was möchtest du später werden?
Antonio: Selbständig möcht' ich werden.
Sonja: Was interessiert dich an deinem Beruf?
Antonio: Nun, der Kontakt mit den Gästen und es macht mir einfach Spaß.
Sonja: Gibt es etwas, was dich stört?
Antonio: Die langen Arbeitszeiten und wenig Freizeit.
Sonja: Was möchtest du später werden?
Brigitte: Ich möchte Restaurantfachfrau werden.
Sonja: Und warum?
Brigitte: Weil ich sehr viel Spaß an diesem Beruf habe und viel mit Leuten in Kontakt komme.

(at a brewery school)
Sonja: Was möchtest du später werden?
Michael: Brauer.
Sonja: Was reizt dich an dem Beruf?
Michael: Die verschiedenen Naturwissenschaften.
Sonja: Welche Ausbildung brauchst du dafür?
Michael: Eine dreijährige Lehre.

E. **Alles klar?** Answer each of the following questions. Write complete sentences.

1. Was können die Schüler nach ihrer gastronomischen Ausbildung machen?
2. Was für einen Schulabschluß hat Antonio?
3. Was gefällt Antonio an seinem Beruf?
4. Was stört ihn daran?
5. Warum möchte Brigitte Restaurantfachfrau werden?
6. Was möchte Michael werden?
7. Was interessiert ihn an diesem Beruf?
8. Welche Ausbildung braucht man, wenn man Brauer werden will?

F. **FÜR ZWEI ODER GRUPPEN: Schule und Berufsausbildung**

Discuss with your partner(s) education and professional training in Germany and in the United States.

- What have you learned from this program that you didn't know before?
- What are the differences in education and professional training between Germany and the United States?
- What do you think are the advantages/disadvantages of each system?
- Where would you rather go to school? Why?

Cultural Note

In Germany almost all labor is skilled. To become certified the apprentices have to complete a three to three and a half year training program. If you want to work as a mechanic, hairdresser, or electrician, you have to be certified. Only certified master craftsmen are allowed to run a shop. To become a certified master craftsman, the skilled worker has to pass a test (**Meisterprüfung**) after an additional two-year training period. These strict business regulations were instituted by the guilds and have had a large impact on German society as a whole. For example, Germans don't change occupations as frequently as Americans, because they would have to start at the bottom again and undergo a three-year training period. This means that Germans tend to stick with their profession, or even the same company, until they retire at the age of 65.

Sonja: Macht die Ausbildung Spaß?
Stefan: Macht Spaß, ja.
Sonja: Ist es leicht, später eine Anstellung zu finden?
Stefan: In diesem Zweig gibt es sehr viele Stellen, offene Stellen.
Sonja: Wieviel wirst du am Anfang ungefähr verdienen?
Stefan: Ich werde verdienen auf die Hand knappe 2000 Mark.
Sonja: Können auch Mädchen Brauer werden?
Stefan: Ja, es gibt Mädchen, aber es sind sehr wenige, leider.
Sonja: Was möchtest du werden?
Rainer: Brauer.
Sonja: Was interessiert dich an dem Beruf?
Rainer: Ja, vor allem die chemisch-physikalischen Vorgänge und überhaupt die ganze Arbeit.
Sonja: Wie lange dauert die Ausbildung?
Rainer: Die dauert 3 Jahre, an der Berufsschule.
Sonja: Macht es Spaß?
Rainer: Ja, sehr.

G. **Alles klar?**

1. Als Bierbrauer kann man leicht eine Anstellung finden, weil
   a) die Leute viel Bier trinken b) es viele Stellen gibt
   c) der Beruf vielen Leuten Spaß macht

2. Wieviel wird Stefan am Anfang verdienen?
   a) ungefähr 2000 DM b) mehr als 2000 DM c) viel weniger als 2000 DM

3. Wie viele Mädchen wollen Bierbrauer werden?
   a) viele b) einige c) wenige

4. Rainier interessiert sich für
   a) Mathematik und Physik b) Chemie und Physik c) Mathematik und Chemie

Scene 3: Interviews with Apprentices at BMW

chapter 4 to 5

der **Aufbau** organization
Automobilmechaniker,- car mechanic
Azubi,-s short for **Auszubildende** apprentice
Betrieb,-e company
Lehrling,-e apprentice
Mechaniker,- mechanic

die **Eigenschaft,-en** quality, characteristic
Fingerfertigkeit manual dexterity
Technik technology

reparieren to repair
übernehmen (übernimmt), übernommen to take over

abwechslungsreich diverse
im Außendienst on service call
ich habe mit ... zu tun I have to deal with...

Grammar

In the active voice the subject of the sentence performs the action described by the verb. This subject is the agent or "doer".

Example:

Active: **Die Berufsschule bildet die Lehrlinge aus.**

In the passive voice the subject is acted upon. The agent or doer that performs the action is generally introduced by the active preposition **von**. The object which is acted upon in the active voice sentences becomes the subject of the passive voice sentence.

Passive: **Die Lehrlinge werden von der Berufsschule ausgebildet.**

Not all sentences in the passive voice contain an agent. The passive voice uses a form of **werden** and a past participle.

An dieser Schule werden die Schüler zu gastronomischen Berufen ausgebildet.
In this school the students are being trained for gastronomy.

In München werden BMWs produziert.
In Munich BMWs are produced.

Es werden ziemlich viele Zahnarzthelferinnen gesucht.
Quite a number of dental hygienists are being sought.

On Screen

München ist der Geburtsort von BMW. Im Münchner Werk werden Autos der 3-er Reihe und Motoren produziert. Hier werden auch 900 Lehrlinge in 33 verschiedenen Berufen ausgebildet. 93% der Azubis werden in den Betrieb übernommen.

Munich is the birthplace of the BMW. In the Munich plant cars of the "3-series" (a special model) are produced. Nine hundred apprentices are also being trained in thirty-three different professions. Ninety-three percent of these apprentices will later be employed by the company.

H. **Watch and listen!** Fill in the blanks as you watch the video.

Sonja: Was für eine Ausbildung machst du hier?

Heiner: Ich lern' hier ______________________________.
Sonja: Wie lange dauert die Ausbildung?

Heiner: Die dauert 3-1/2 _______________.

Sonja: Was interessiert dich an dem Beruf?

Manfred: An meinem _______________ interessiert mich, daß ich mit Autos zu tun habe, daß ich _______________ repariere.
Sonja: Braucht man besondere Eigenschaften dazu?
Manfred: Man braucht 'n bißchen Fingerfertigkeit und man muß sich für den Beruf ___________________.
Sonja: Wie findest du BMWs?

Manfred: Ja, BMW find' ich___________________ — toll.

Sonja: Was möchtest du später werden?

Wolfgang: ___________________ bei BMW im Außendienst.
Sonja: Und was interessiert dich besonders daran?

Wolfgang: Die ___________________ und der ganze Aufbau.
Sonja: Was für eine Ausbildung brauchst du dafür?

Wolfgang: Die Lehrzeit dauert ___________________ Jahre bei BMW.
Sonja: Macht dir diese Ausbildung Spaß?

Wolfgang: Ja, weil es ist ___________________ und abwechslungsreich.
Sonja: Wieviel wirst du am Anfang verdienen?

Wolfgang: Um die ________________________________.
Sonja: Was findest du besonders gut am BMW?
Wolfgang: Ja die Technik, der Aufbau.
Sonja: Möchtest du später selbst einen fahren?
Wolfgang: Wenn das Geld reicht. (If I have enough money.)

On Screen

Mehr als 4 Millionen BMWs fahren heute auf der ganzen Welt. Hinzu kommen 400.000 Motorräder.
There are over 4 million BMWs all over the world. In addition there are 400,000 motorbikes.

I. **Alles klar**? Answer the following questions. Write complete sentences.

1. Was wird bei BMW in München produziert?
2. Wer wird hier ausgebildet?
3. Wie viele Azubis werden später in den Betrieb übernommen?
4. Wie lange dauert eine Ausbildung zum Automobilmechaniker?
5. Warum gefällt Heiner und Wolfgang diese Ausbildung?
6. Wieviel verdient ein Automobilmechaniker nach der Ausbildung?

J. **Übung**. Convert the following sentences from active to passive voice.

Example: Das Münchner Werk produziert BMWs der 3-Reihe.
BMWs der 3-Reihe werden vom Münchner Werk produziert.

1. Das Werk bildet auch 900 Lehrlinge aus.
2. Die Lehrlinge reparieren die Autos.
3. Der Betrieb übernimmt 93% der Azubis.
4. Mehr als 4 Millionen BMWs fahren heute auf der ganzen Welt.

chapter 5 to 6

Scene 4: Interviews with Students at a Dental School

der **Lärm** noise
Ratschlag,¨-e advice
Streß stress
Zahnarzt,¨-e dentist (m.)
Zahntechniker,- dental technician (m.)

die **Belastung,-en** burden, stress, pollution
Chemikalie,-n chemical
Gesamtarbeitszeit total time at work
Praxis here: office
Überstunde,-n overtime
Zahnarzthelferin,-nen dental assistant (f.)
Zahnärztin,-nen dentist (f.)

das **Erfolgserlebnis,-se** accomplishment, achievement

auf/nehmen (nimmt auf) to absorb
behalten (behält) to keep
ein/atmen (atmet ein) to breathe in, absorb
höchstens at the highest, at the most
manuell manual
unter der Woche during the week

K. **Watch and listen!** Fill in the blanks as you watch the video.

Sonja: Dies ist die Berufsschule für Zahnarzthelferinnen und Zahntechniker. Die Schüler arbeiten 4 Tage in der Woche in der ____________ und müssen einmal in der Woche zum Unterricht in die ____________ .

Sonja: Was willst du später werden?

Bettina: ________________________ .
Sonja: Was reizt dich besonders daran?
Bettina: Die Erfolgserlebnisse.
Sonja: Was für eine Ausbildung brauchst du?

Bettina Eine ________________ Berufsschulausbildung.
Sonja: Macht dir die Ausbildung Spaß?

Bettina Ja, ____________.
Sonja: Gibt es etwas, was dich stört?

Bettina: Vielleicht die vielen ______________ .
Sonja: Meinst du, es wird leicht sein, später eine Anstellung zu finden?

Bettina Ja, weil es ______________ ziemlich viele Zahnarzthelferinnen gesucht.

Sonja: Hier scheinen nur Mädchen zu sein — sind hier auch einige ____________?

Bettina: Ich denke schon, aber es gibt nur sehr, sehr ______________.
Sonja: Welchen Ratschlag würdest du uns geben, um gute Zähne zu behalten?

Bettina Daß man sie nach jedem ____________ putzt.

Sonja: Macht dir die Ausbildung Spaß?

Ruth: Ja, es____________.
Sonja: Was stört dich daran?
Ruth: Daß die Gesamtarbeitszeit auch bei den Auszubildenden unter der Woche zu lang ist und daß es zu wenig ____________ gibt.
Sonja: Was interessiert dich an diesem Beruf?

Gabi: Daß ich anderen ____________ helfen kann.
Sonja: Ist es leicht, später eine Anstellung zu finden?
Gabi: Ja, doch, eigentlich schon.
Sonja: Wieviel wirst du am Anfang ungefähr verdienen?

Gabi: Mei, ____________ netto höchstens.

On Screen

Dies sind die zukünftigen Zahntechniker. Ihre Ausbildung dauert 3-1/2 Jahre.
These are future dental technicians. Their training period lasts three and a half years.

Sonja: Was findest du an diesem Beruf ____________________?

Horst: Ich finde gut diese sehr vielfältige Arbeit und die manuelle ____________________.

Sonja: Gibt es etwas, was dich stört?

Horst: Die Belastung durch __________ und Chemikalien durch das Einatmen und auch was man auf den, in den __________ aufnimmt.

Sonja: Was für einen Schulabschluß hast du?

Torsten: Ich hab' die Mittlere ____________ und mach' eine dreijährige Ausbildung zum ____________________.

Sonja: Und macht es dir Spaß?

Torsten: Ja, sehr.

Sonja: Stört dich etwas?

Torsten: Ja, der ___________.

L. **<u>Alles klar</u>? Was reizt, interessiert oder gefällt den jungen Zahnarzthelferinnen und Zahntechnikern an ihrem Beruf und was stört sie daran? Machen Sie eine Liste!**

Example:	**positiv**	**negativ**
Antonio:	**Kontakt mit Menschen**	**wenig Freizeit**
Bettina:		
Ruth:		
Gabi:		
Horst:		
Torsten:		

M. Now form as many sentences as possible with the information that you collected above. Create at least one sentence for each person.

Example

Antonio	**interessiert** **reizt** **stört**	**an**	**seiner Ausbilding,**		
			daß er...	**Kontakt mit Menschen** **zu wenig Freizeit** **nicht genug Geld**	**hat.** **verdient.**

N. **FÜR ZWEI**

Was reizt Sie und was stört Sie an Ihrem Studium, Ihrer Ausbildung oder Ihrem späteren Beruf? Talk to your partner about what you like and don't like about your education, or future career.

Model

A:	**Was**	**interessiert** **reizt** **stört**	**dich an**	**deinem späteren Beruf?** **deiner Ausbildung?**
B:	**Mich**	"	**daran, daß ...**	

Cultural Note

In Germany there is still a traditional gender bias in many professions. For example, you will find very few female bus drivers, lawyers or doctors. In elementary education, in the social services such as nursing, or in the garment industry, women are in the majority. Generally women are employed in lower-paying professions.

Scene 5: Interviews at a School for Fashion Designers

chapter 6 to 7

der Stoff,-e material

die Meisterprüfung,-en master's exam (vocational)
Meisterschule,-n school for master students
Seide silk

das Fach,¨-er subject, field
Kostüm,-e costume
Material,-ien material

an/fertigen (fertigt an) to make, produce
entwerfen to design
kombinieren to combine
kriegen = bekommen to get

angestellt employed

aufwendig lavish, costly
ins Ausland abroad
nach einer gewissen Zeit after a certain time
vor allem (v.a.) especially, above all
würd' ich schon sagen I would say so

künstlerisch artistic, creative

immerzu = immer always
motiviert motivated

zu Gast sein to visit

O. **Watch and listen!** Fill in the blanks as you watch the video.

Sonja: Nun sind wir zu Gast bei der Deutschen Meisterschule für Mode. Hier werden 300 Schülerinnen und Schüler zu modisch-künstlerischen Berufen ausgebildet. Now we are visiting the German Master School for Fashion, where 300 students are educated in fashion design.

Sonja: Was für eine Ausbildung machst du hier?

Regine: Ich mach' die Ausbildung zur ________________________.
Sonja: Was möchtest du später werden?
Regine: Später, nach einer gewissen Zeit, wo ich noch angestellt bin, möcht' ich mich

__________________machen.

Sonja: Wie lange dauert die Ausbildung?

Martina: _________________ Jahre.

Sonja: Und welche Fächer machen dir am meisten Spaß?

Martina: Die praktischen ________________.
Sonja: Sag' mal, braucht man besondere Eigenschaften für diesen Beruf?

Martina: Würd' ich schon sagen, man muß einfach Fingerfertigkeit ________________.

Sonja: Was entwirfst du am liebsten?
Ulla: Am liebsten Abendkleider und Cocktailkleider, denn das

__________________ gefällt mir sehr gut, die Seide und aufwendige Sachen.

Sonja: Was fertigst du am liebsten an?

Daniela: __________________, weil man sie so wunderbar kombinieren kann.
Sonja: Ist es nicht schwer, immerzu neue Ideen zu haben?

Daniela: Doch das ist schon sehr __________________, vor allem wenn man nicht richtig motiviert ist.
Sonja: Woher bekommst du deine Ideen?

Daniela: Das ist ganz unterschiedlich, manchmal auf der __________________ oder aus Zeitungen oder wenn man einen Stoff sieht.
Sonja: Wirst du später leicht eine Anstellung finden?
Daniela: Ich hoffe schon, aber man weiß es nie, ob man das genau kriegt was man sich

______________________.

Sonja: Wirst du hier in München bleiben oder könntest du auch ins Ausland gehen?

Daniela: Man kann sicherlich auch ins ______________________ gehen.
Sonja: Und möchtest du das?
Daniela: Ich würde gerne nach Hong Kong ______________________.

P. Alles klar? Answer the following questions in complete sentences.

1. Wie viele Schülerinnen und Schüler werden von der deutschen Meisterschule ausgebildet?

2. Was müssen die Schülerinnen und Schüler am Ende ihrer Ausbildung machen?

3. Wie lange dauert die Ausbildung?

4. Welche besonderen Eigenschaften braucht man für den Beruf der Modedesignerin?

5. Was entwirft Ulla am liebsten?

6. Was fertigt Daniela am liebsten an?

7. Woher bekommt Daniela ihre Ideen?

8. Wie sehen Danielas Zukunftpläne aus?

Q. **Und Sie? Haben Sie auch Zukunftspläne?** Talk to your partner about your plans for the future.

Model

A: Was würdest du gern / am liebsten nach der Ausbildung machen?

B: Ich würde gern...

A: Wirst du später leicht eine Anstellung finden?

B: Es ist (nicht) sehr schwer, weil....
Ich hoffe schon, aber...

R. **FÜR ZWEI**

Think about twenty years from now. You are in the midst of your professional career and a reporter comes to you and asks

- what kind of job you have
- what you have to do
- what educational and professional training you needed
- what personal qualities and skills you need
- what you like about your profession and what you don't like
- if you have colleagues and how you get along with them
- how much money you make
- what is the most important thing for you about your career.

PROGRAMM 18

FILM, FUNK UND FERNSEHEN

This episode informs us about the German radio, TV, and motion picture industry. We visit a Bavarian TV studio, where Sonja asks several employees about their jobs. Interviews with people from all walks of life tell us about German TV-watching habits. We also go on a tour of the Bavaria Film Studio, where we see several stuntmen in action. We also meet the anchorwoman of a popular private radio station, and finally we visit a photography school.

Susanne, Radio Xanadu

LANGUAGE FUNCTIONS

- talking about habits and intellectual interests
- talking about job requirements
- describing personal skills, strengths and weaknesses

CONTENTS

- German TV and Radio
- German film industry
- professional training
- complex sentences

chapter 7 to 16

Scene 1: Interview with Bavarian TV News Announcer

chapter 8 to 9

der Nachrichtensprecher,- newscaster, anchorman

die Aussprache,-n pronunciation
Bevölkerung population
Bevölkerungsschicht,-en segment of population
Nachricht,-en news
Nachrichtensprecherin,-nen anchorwoman
Sprecherausbildung speech training
Stelle,-n place, spot

ein/treffen (trifft ein) to arrive
über etwas verfügen = etwas besitzen to possess something; to be in charge of something

als erstes at first
tagespolitische Ereignisse latest political events

Sonja: Was sind Sie von Beruf?
Martin: Ich bin Nachrichtensprecher.
Sonja: Was für eine Ausbildung braucht man dazu?
Martin: Man braucht auf jeden Fall eine Sprecherausbildung und sollte auch über Abitur verfügen.
Sonja: Finden Sie Ihren Beruf interessant?
Martin: Ja, man sitzt auf jeden Fall an der Stelle, wo die tagespolitischen Ereignisse als erstes eintreffen.
Sonja: Was für besondere Eigenschaften braucht man?
Martin: Man sollte attraktiv für eine breite Bevölkerungsschicht sein und eine gute Aussprache besitzen.

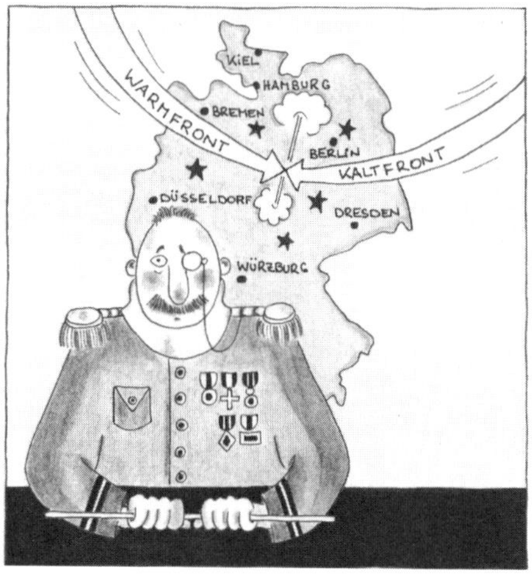

Cultural Note

In Germany the style of presenting the news is dry. In contrast to the United States, where the newscaster interviews news correspondents on the show, the typical German newscaster simply reads the news. It would be completely inappropriate for a German newscaster to joke with the other members of the news team. Weather predictions and sports events, just like all the other news items, are simply announced in a very factual, serious manner.

chapter 9 to 10

Scene 2: How Much TV Do You Watch Every Day?

der **Bereich,-e** field, area
Fernseher,- TV set
Rundfunk radio
Streit,-e argument, fight
Zuschauer,- viewer

das **Abendbrot = das Abendessen** supper
Programm,-e channel

fern/schauen (schaut fern) = fern/sehen (sieht fern) to watch TV
gucken = kucken coll.: to watch

ungefähr approximately

gucken is only used in spoken German. When writing you would either use **sehen** or **schauen**. The question that Sonja asks could be rephrased in writing:

Wie oft schauen Sie fern? oder **Wieviel Zeit verbringen Sie vor dem Fernseher?**

Sonja: Grüß Gott, liebe Zuschauer! Wir sind in den Fernsehstudios des Bayrischen Rundfunks, und es geht um Film und Fernsehen. In dieser Folge werden wir Leute kennenlernen, die in diesem Bereich arbeiten. Doch zuerst wollte ich wissen: Wieviel Fernsehen guckst du am Tag?

Luca: Nicht viel — pro Tag gucke ich vielleicht eine Stunde.
Sonja: Und mit wem guckst du Fernsehen? Mit deiner Familie?
Luca: Meistens alleine.

Sonja: Wieviel Fernsehen guckst du?
Jan: Ich schau' nicht sehr viel fern; ich hab' nicht besonders viel' Zeit fernzuschauen, ich hab' viele andere Hobbies.

A **Und Sie? Wieviel Fernsehen gucken Sie am Tag?** How much TV do you watch every day? **Gibt es manchmal Streit um das Programm?** Do you sometimes argue about channels?

B. **Make a list about the TV habits of the interviewed people.**

	Wieviel Fernsehen gucken sie?	Mit wem schauen sie fern?
Luca:	____________	____________
Jan:	____________	____________
Vanessa:	____________	____________
Heike:	____________	____________
Udo:	____________	____________
Antje:	____________	____________
Bernd:	____________	____________

Glauben Sie, daß die Amerikaner mehr Zeit vor dem Fernseher verbringen als die Deutschen?

Scene 3: Interviews with Employees in a Bavarian TV Studio

chapter 10 to 11

der Bildmischer,- video mixer
Bildspeicher,- picture storage unit
Schriftgenerator,-en titling machine
Ton,¨-e sound
Toningenieur,-e sound engineer

die Elektrotechnik electronics
Fachhochschule,-n four-year college
Fähigkeit,-en ability
Hälfte,-n one-half
Spannung,-en tension, suspense
Verbindung,-en (zwischen) connection (between) here: combination

bedienen to operate
ein/lernen (lernt ein) to train on the job

abwechslungsreich varied
geregelt regular, formal
vielseitig multifaceted
an sich actually
im Haus here: on the job
in erster Linie above all, in the first place

Sonja: Ein kurzer Blick hinter die Kulissen des Bayrischen Rundfunks. Im Kontrollraum bereiten Redakteure und Techniker die 17-Uhr-Nachrichten vor.
A short glimpse behind the scenes of the Bavarian public broadcasting station. In the control room journalists and technicians prepare the 5 o'clock evening news.

Sonja: Was sind Sie von Beruf?
Matthias: Ich bin Bildmischer.
Sonja: Welche Ausbildung braucht man dafür?
Matthias: Es gibt keine geregelte. Ich hab' das hier anderthalb Jahre im Haus gelernt — beim Bayerischen Rundfunk.
Sonja: Finden Sie Ihren Beruf interessant?
Matthias: Ja sehr, er ist vielseitig und abwechslungsreich.

Sonja: Was sind Sie von Beruf?
Olaf: Ich bediene den Schriftgenerator und den Bildspeicher.
Sonja: Welche Ausbildung braucht man dazu?
Olaf: Man braucht keine Ausbildung; man wird eingelernt.
Sonja: Finden Sie Ihren Beruf interessant?

Olaf:	Ja, ich find's sehr interessant. Mich interessiert die Spannung in der Live-Sendung.
Sonja:	Was für besondere Fähigkeiten braucht man?
Olaf:	Man braucht an sich keine.
Sonja:	Können das auch Frauen machen?
Olaf:	Ja, die Hälfte von uns sind Frauen.
Sonja:	Wieviel verdienen Sie?
Olaf:	Ich verdiene 300 Mark am Abend.

Sonja:	Was sind Sie von Beruf?
Rüdiger:	Ich bin Toningenieur.
Sonja:	Was für eine Ausbildung braucht man?
Rüdiger:	Man studiert Musik und Elektrotechnik an einer Fachhochschule.
Sonja:	Finden Sie Ihren Beruf interessant?
Rüdiger:	Ich find' ihn sehr interessant, ja.
Sonja:	Und warum?
Rüdiger:	Mich reizt die Verbindung zwischen Musik und Technik vor allem.
Sonja:	Was für Eigenschaften braucht man für Ihren Beruf?
Rüdiger:	Man sollte eigentlich in erster Linie musikalisch sein.

C. **Alles klar? Was sind sie von Beruf und welche Ausbildung haben sie? Machen Sie eine Liste.**

	Beruf	**Ausbildung**
Matthias:	____________________	____________________
Olaf:	____________________	____________________
Rüdiger:	____________________	____________________

D. Answer the following questions in complete sentences using the conjunction **weil**.

1. Matthias findet seinen Beruf interessant, weil

   ____

2. Olaf findet seinen Beruf interessant, weil

   ____

3. Rüdiger findet seinen Beruf interessant, weil

   ____

Scene 4: Bavaria Stuntshow

chapter 11 to 12

der Krieg,-e war
Normalbürger,- average person
Spielfilm,-e feature film
Stuntman stuntman
Weltkrieg,-e world war

die Filmbranche,-n film industry
Filmtourführerin,-nen film tour leader
Führerin,-nen leader
Voraussetzung,-en precondition

das Filmstudio,-s
Gelände,- area
Filmgelände,- film area
U-Boot,-e submarine

an etwas kommen to get something
einen Film drehen to shoot a movie
einen Test machen to take a test
führen to lead
handeln von to deal with
hinter die Kulissen schauen to see behind the scenes
mit/machen (macht mit) to take part in, participate
um/gehen mit (geht um) to deal with, to cope with
Umgang haben mit to deal with, to be in touch with
Wie bist du an deinen Job gekommen? How did you get your job?

berühmt famous
fertig finished
humorvoll witty, humorous
reizvoll intriguing
bestimmt certain
gesamt whole, total
im Schnitt on the average
selbstbewußt self-confident

Sonja: Wir sind in den Bavaria Film-Studios. Hier werden Spielfilme, Fernsehfilme und Videoclips produziert. Ich mache jetzt einmal die Tour mit.
We are in the Bavaria Film Studios. Feature films, TV films, and video clips are being produced here. I'll take part in the tour first.

(on a submarine boat set)
In diesem U-Boot wurde der berühmte Film "Das Boot" gedreht. Er wurde 1981 nach jahrelanger Arbeit fertig und kostete 30 Millionen Mark. Der Film handelt von Ereignissen auf einem U-Boot während des Zweiten Weltkriegs.

The famous movie "**Das Boot**" was filmed in this submarine. It was finished in 1981 after years of work at a cost of 30 Million Marks. The film deals with events on a submarine during World War II.

Sonja: Was ist dein Job hier?
Heike: Ich bin Filmtourführerin, das heißt, daß ich hier die Touristen über das Filmgelände führe.
Sonja: Wie bist du an deinen Job gekommen?
Heike: Man bekommt hier eine dreitägige Ausbildung, und dann muß man einen Test machen, und wenn man gut ist, dann wird man genommen und kann hier arbeiten.
Sonja: Und findest du deinen Job interessant?
Heike: Ja, sehr interessant, weil ich viele Leute kennenlerne, viel mit Leuten Umgang hab', und das mag ich sehr gern.

On Screen

Internationale Stars wie Steve McQueen, Elizabeth Taylor und Richard Burton haben hier Filme gedreht.
International stars like Steve McQueen, Elizabeth Taylor and Richard Burton have made films here.

Sonja: Was sind Sie von Beruf?
Antje: Moderatorin.
Sonja: Braucht man eine bestimmte Ausbildung?
Antje: Keine bestimmte, man muß gut reden können.
Sonja: Was finden Sie an Ihrem Beruf besonders interessant?
Antje: Mit Menschen umzugehen.
Sonja: Was für besondere Charaktereigenschaften braucht man?
Antje: Man muß selbstbewußt sein und auch humorvoll.
Sonja: Wieviel verdienen Sie ungefähr im Monat?
Antje: Zwischen 3000 und 4000 Mark.

Sonja: Was ist Ihr Beruf?
Udo: Stuntman.
Sonja: Welche Eigenschaften braucht man dafür?
Udo: Man muß sehr sportlich sein.
Sonja: Was finden Sie an Ihrem Beruf besonders interessant?
Udo: Daß man als Normalbürger auch mal hinter die Kulissen schauen kann.
Sonja: Können auch Frauen Stunts machen?
Udo: In Deutschland weniger — in Amerika ist die Chance viel größer.
Sonja: Wieviel verdienen sie normalerweise im Monat?
Udo: Ich würde sagen, im Schnitt 8000 Mark.

Sonja: Was sind Sie von Beruf?
Rolf: Ich bin Stuntman von Beruf.
Sonja: Welche Eigenschaften braucht man dazu?
Rolf: Wichtige Voraussetzung: man sollte sehr sportlich sein.
Sonja: Was finden Sie an Ihrem Beruf besonders reizvoll?
Rolf: Ich glaube, daß in diesem Beruf die gesamte Filmbranche sehr interessant ist, einfach mal die Möglichkeit zu haben, hinter die Kulissen zu schauen.

E. **Alles klar?**

1. Wo wurde "Das Boot" gedreht?
2. Wann wurde der Film fertig und wieviel hat er gekostet?
3. Wovon handelt der Film "Das Boot"?
4. Wieviel verdient ein Stuntman im Monat?
5. Was ist besonders reizvoll an diesem Beruf?

F. Make a list.

	Welchen Beruf haben sie?	**Welche Eigenschaften braucht man?**
Antje:	______________________	______________________
Udo:	______________________	______________________
Rolf:	______________________	______________________

	Welche Ausbildung braucht man?	**Warum ist der Beruf interessant?**
Heike:	______________________	______________________
Sonja:	______________________	______________________

Scene 5: German Television

der **Kanal,⸚e** channel
Krimi,-s detective story
Horrorfilm,-e horror movie

die **Auswahl (an)** + dat. choice
Lieblingssendung,-en favorite program
Riesenauswahl (an + dat.) enormous choice (of)
Serie,-n series
Unterhaltung entertainment

das **Fernsehprogramm,-e** TV channel
Kabelfernsehen cable TV

da bin ich überfragt I don't know

Sonja: In Deutschland gibt es eine Riesenauswahl an Fernsehprogrammen. Ich wollte wissen wie viele.

Sonja: Wie viele Fernsehprogramme gibt es in Deutschland?
Rolf: Da bin ich überfragt — viel zu viel wahrscheinlich.

Luca: Also speziell bei uns im Hause, wir haben Kabelfernsehen, wir haben 23 Kanäle.

Sonja: Wie viele Fernsehkanäle gibt es in Deutschland?
Miriam: So 10 oder 15.

Petra: Ziemlich viele, vielleicht bis 20 ungefähr.

Cultural Note

Kabelfernsehen was introduced in Germany in the 1980s. Since then TV has become more uniform, because many of the cable programs, such as MTV, can be received all over the world. In contrast to the United States, Germany still has three national public broadcast channels (**ARD, ZDF, Drittes Programm**) that do not depend on donations, but are financed with mandatory TV owners' fees and tax subsidies. The program decisions of these public broadcasting channels are made by supervisory boards which are influenced by public interest groups such as political parties and mass media representatives. Because these advisory boards hold strong political power, there have been many public debates about the danger of political indoctrination of the audience.

Note: **Programm** means channel, **Sendung** means program.

G. **FÜR GRUPPEN: Eine eigene Fernsehsendung**

You are asked to do a new show for German television. It can be any type of program: a program that you like on American TV, a variation of one or a completely new show. Develop an outline of the show together. Talk about:

- What is the title of the program?
- What is it about?
- What kind of program is it (education, entertainment,...)?
- For what audience is it intended (age group, daytime,...)?
- What is special about the program and why will people want to watch it?

Scene 6: Favorite TV Programs

chapter 13 to 14

Sonja: Hier in meinem Hotelzimmer gibt es 22 Programme. Ich schau' mir am liebsten Spielfilme und Krimis an. Von anderen Leuten wollte ich wissen: Was sind deine Lieblingssendungen?

H. **Alles klar? Was sind ihre Lieblingssendungen?**

Vanessa: ______________________ **Udo:** ______________________

Heike: ______________________ **Jan:** ______________________

Luca: ______________________ **Tina:** ______________________

Nicole: ______________________

I. **FÜR ZWEI**

Was sind Ihre Lieblingssendungen?

Beispiel: Ich schau' mir am liebsten Dallas an. Ich finde die Sendung unterhaltsam (entertaining).

Ich schau' mir	**am liebsten...** **nie...**		
	Krimis		**interessant**
	Nachrichtensendungen		**toll**
	Spielfilme	**an.**	**blöd**
	Sportsendungen		**langweilig**
	Dokumentarfilme		**entspannend**
	Werbung		**unterhaltsam**
	Musiksendungen		
	Horrorfilme		
	Raumschiff Enterprise		
	Quizsendungen		
	?		

Was halten Sie vom amerikanischen Fernsehen? (What is your opinion about American TV?) Create sentences according to the example below.

Beispiel: **Ich bin der Meinung, daß es zu viel Brutalität gibt.**

Ich	**finde (nicht),...** **glaube (nicht),...** **bin (nicht) der Meinung,...**		
daß es	**zu viel** **zu wenig** **(nicht) wenig**	**Programme** **Sportsendungen** **Musiksendungen** **Brutalität** (violence) **Werbung** **Kultur** **Politik**	**gibt.**

Scene 7: Do You Listen to the Radio?

chapter 14 to 15

der **Bayrische Rundfunk** Bavarian Public Radio
Sender,- station
Zuhörer,- listener
Zuhörerkreis,-e listening audience

die **Rundfunkstation, -en** broadcasting station
das **Fernsehpublikum** TV audience
Radio Xanadu name of a Munich radio station

halten von + dat. to think of
vergleichen mit to compare to

eine Platte auf/legen (legt auf) to put on a record
gelegentlich occasionally
kritisch critical
relativ relatively
im Hintergrund in the background
öffentlichrechtlich public
unabhängig independent

Sonja: Film und Fernsehen sind natürlich extrem populär. Aber auch das Radio spielt eine wichtige Rolle. In München gibt es mehrere Radiostationen wie z.B. Radio Xanadu, das richtig zum Straßenbild dazugehört.

Movies and TV are of course very popular. But radio also plays an important role. In Munich there are several radio stations, such as **Radio Xanadu,** which is part of the Munich street scene.

Sonja: Was für Sendungen machen Sie?

Susanne: Ich moderiere hauptsächlich Informations- und Unterhaltungssendungen

Sonja: Wie viele Rundfunkstationen gibt es in München?

Susanne: In München gibt es 5 private Rundfunkstationen und eine öffentlichrechtliche, den Bayrischen Rundfunk mit 4 Programmen.

Sonja: Hören Sie selbst auch gern Radio?

Susanne: Wenn ich Radio höre, Radio Xanadu. Ansonsten leg ich lieber eine Platte auf.

Sonja: Susannes Zuhörerkreis ist relativ klein, wenn man ihn mit dem Fernsehpublikum vergleicht. Ich fragte einige Leute, was sie vom Radio halten.

Sonja: Hörst du ab und zu auch Radio?

Oskar: Hauptsächlich. Mehr als Fernsehen.

Sonja: Wann hörst du Radio?

Oskar: Eigentlich läuft's immer neben der Arbeit oder bei der Arbeit im Hintergrund.

Sonja: Was ist deine Lieblingsstation?

Oskar: Radio Xanadu.

Sonja: Warum?

Oskar: Die sind unabhängig, sind sehr kritisch und bringen sehr gute Musik.

Sonja: Hörst du ab und zu Radio?

Annette: Ja.

Sonja: Und wann?

Annette: Morgens, abends.

Sonja: Was hörst du?

Annette: Radio Gong 2000.

Sonja: Hörst du ab und zu auch Radio?

Holger: Ja, schon.

Sonja: Zu welcher Tageszeit?

Holger: Hauptsächlich morgens.

Sonja: Was ist dein Lieblingssender?

Holger: Radio Xanadu.

Sonja: Was gefällt dir dran?

Holger: Daß nicht soviel gesprochen wird wie auf den anderen Sendern.

Sonja: Hörst du auch mal Radio?

Ulrich: Nein, nie.

Joachim: Gelegentlich.

Sonja: Und was?

Joachim: Meistens Nachrichtensendungen.

J. <u>Alles klar</u>?

1. Susanne arbeitet für
   a) den Bayrischen Rundfunk b) das deutsche Fernsehen c) Radio Xanadu

2. Radio Xanadu ist
   a) eine Unterhaltungssendung b) eine private Rundfunkstation
   c) eine öffentliche Rundfunkstation

3. Susanne hört
   a) manchmal Radio b) immer Radio c) nie Radio

4. Radio Xanadu hat
   a) keine Zuhörer b) mehr Zuhörer als das Fernsehen
   c) weniger Zuhörer als das Fernsehen

5. **Wie oft hören sie Radio?**

	immer	**oft**	**manchmal**	**selten**	**nie**
Oskar:	________	________	________	________	________
Annette:	________	________	________	________	________
Holger:	________	________	________	________	________
Ulrich:	________	________	________	________	________
Joachim:	________	________	________	________	________

Susanne DJ
Radio Xanadu

Scene 8: A Visit to a Photography School

der Apparat,-e apparatus, contraption
Fotograf,-en photographer
Kameramann,¨-er camera operator

die Anstellung,-en job, position
Cutterin,-nen film editor
Fotografie,-n photography
Fotografin,-nen photographer
Industrie free enterprise
Presse press
Werbung marketing

das Auffassungsvermögen perception
Handwerk skill, craft

etwas fotografieren to take pictures of
etwas verändern to change something
meinen to think
tätig sein to be active, work

alltäglich everyday
beruflich professional
sogar even
speziell special
technisch technical, mechanical

eine Übung machen to do an exercise
zu tun haben mit to deal with

L. Alles klar? Answer the following questions.

Was möchten sie später werden? Machen Sie eine Liste!

Renate: ______________________ **Ulrich:** ______________________

Annette: ______________________ **Holger:** ______________________

Was gefällt den Schülern besonders an ihrem Beruf? Use your own words and write complete sentences about their professional motivation.

Renate: *Renate gefällt besonders an ihrem Beruf, daß* ____________________

____

Ulrich: ____

____

Annette: ____

____

Holger: ____

____

L. **FÜR ZU HAUSE: Filmkritik**

Write a review about a movie for a German newspaper. Talk about:

- What the movie is about.
- What are the main characteristics of the story and people?
- How did you like the actors; were they believable? Why (not)?
- How did you like the direction?
- Do you recommend the movie? Why (not)?
- How many stars do you give it? (*=bad, ****=excellent)

Kids from film school

PROGRAMM 19

SOLDAT ODER ZIVI?

In this episode we learn about the duties of German soldiers as well as those who choose to perform community service as an alternative to military service. First Sonja introduces us to a special army division of mountaineers and interviews them about their daily lives. Then we get a chance to meet a conscientious objector and learn about his work with severely handicapped children.

"Zivi" Klaus Keller

LANGUAGE FUNCTIONS

- expressing obligation
- intentions
- personal opinions
- making contrary-to-fact suggestions (subjunctive with **würde**)
- talking about one's personal daily schedule

CONTENTS

- life in the German military service
- life as a conscientious objector
- attitudes toward war and peace

chapter 1 to 5

Scene 1: Choosing Military or Civilian Service

chapter 2 to 3

Cultural Note

Germany has the draft. All healthy young men who have reached the age of eighteen are required to serve in the German army (**Bundeswehr**) for a minimum of twelve months. If they are opposed to military service for moral, religious or other personal or political reasons, they have the alternative of enlisting as conscientious objectors and doing community service for 18 months (**Zivildienst**). In any case the young men are entitled to complete their high school education or apprenticeship before being drafted.

der **Bund** short for **die Bundeswehr** German army
Soldat,-en soldier
Wohltätigkeitszweck,-e welfare purposes
Zivi,-s short for **Zivildienstleistende,-n** person doing civilian community service
Zivildienst civilian community service
Zweck,-e purpose

die **Bundeswehr** German army
Entscheidung,-en decision
Erfahrung,-en experience
Gewalt violence
Laufbahn,-en career
Verschwendung,-en waste
Waffe,-n weapon
Wohltätigkeit welfare
Zeitverschwendung waste of time

das **Alter,-** age
Militär military
Offizierskasino,-s officers' club

aus/mustern (mustert aus) to discharge from service
benützen to use
erreichen to reach **etwas ab/lehnen (lehnt ab)** to reject or be opposed to something
sich freuen auf to look forward to

die Bundeswehr machen to join the military service
ehrlich honest
eine Entscheidung treffen to make a decision
nichts/viel/nicht viel für etwas übrig haben to think nothing/much/not much of something
wenn ich ehrlich bin... to be honest...

Sonja:	Viele junge Leute müssen, wenn sie mit der Schule fertig sind, außer ihrer beruflichen Laufbahn noch eine andere wichtige Entscheidung treffen—Zivildienst oder Bundeswehr. Ich fragte: Wer muß zur Bundeswehr oder Zivildienst machen? Many young people, once they are finished with school, have to make another important decision—civilian or military service? I asked: Who has to do military service or civilian service?
Luca:	Alle, also alle Jungen, die das Alter von 18 Jahren erreicht haben.
Petra:	Jungen über 18 Jahre.
Sonja:	Würdest du zur Bundeswehr gehen?
Petra	Nein, wenn, dann will ich Zivildienst machen.
Sonja:	Warum?
Petra	Weil ich nicht soviel für Militär übrig habe—also ich finde das nicht so toll.
Sonja:	Würdest du zum Bund gehen?
Monika:	Nicht unbedingt.
Sonja:	Und warum nicht?
Monika:	Weil das Zeitverschwendung ist.
Sonja:	Würdest du zur Bundeswehr gehen?
Nicole:	Nein.
Sonja:	Warum nicht?
Nicole:	Ich lehne das ab—Gewalt und Waffen.
Sonja:	Jungen über 18 müssen entweder 15 Monate zur Bundeswehr oder 20 Monate Zivildienst machen.* Doch nicht jeder freut sich auf diese Erfahrung. Gehst du lieber zur Bundeswehr oder machst du lieber Zivildienst?

* Under new regulations, soldiers now have to serve for a minimum of 12 months. Conscientious objectors have to serve 18 months.

Stefan:	Ich werde die Bundeswehr machen, in 2 Jahren.
Sonja:	Und warum?
Stefan:	Wenn ich ehrlich bin, ist es kürzer. Man verliert weniger Zeit.
Sonja:	Freust du dich darauf?
Stefan:	Eigentlich nicht, nein.
Sonja:	Gehst du später zur Bundeswehr oder machst du Zivildienst?
Michael:	Ich hoff', daß sie mich ausmustern.
Sonja:	Gehst du lieber zum Bund oder machst du Zivildienst?
Antonio:	Ich geh' lieber zum Bund.
Sonja:	Warum?
Antonio:	Ich kann dort in meinem Beruf weitermachen, d.h. in ein Offizierskasino gehen, als Kellner.
Sonja:	Freust du dich schon auf die Zeit?
Antonio:	Nicht besonders.
Sonja:	Wirst du später zur Bundeswehr gehen oder Zivildienst machen?
Bernd:	Lieber Zivildienst.
Sonja:	Warum?
Bernd:	Ich bin gegen Waffen, gegen Gewalt und ich bin der Meinung, man könnte das Geld für Wohltätigkeitszwecke benützen.

Grammar Note

Notice that Sonja interviews the young women first. Since only young men have to join the army or do military service, she asks them a hypothetical question using **würdest**:

> **Würdest du zur Bundeswehr gehen?**

When it is the men's turn she asks in the present tense indicative, because it is not a hypothetical question but a real alternative:

> **Machst du später Zivildienst oder gehst du später zur Bundeswehr?**

Some of the young men interviewed then answer in the future, some in the present tense. Both these tenses can indicate the future.

A. **Alles klar?** List all the reasons people give for joining the military or performing civilian service.

	Bundeswehr oder Zivildienst?	Warum?
Petra:	Zivildienst	Petra hat nicht soviel fürs Militär übrig.
		Sie findet das Militär nicht so toll.
Monika:	______	______
		______
Nicole:	______	______
		______
Stefan:	______	______
		______
Antonio:	______	______
		______
Bernd:	______	______
		______

B. Now take the information on your list and form complete sentences using the conjunction **weil**. Write one sentence for each person. Whenever the alternative is hypothetical (women) you use **würde** (would); when it is real (men) you use present tense or **wird** (will).

Beispiel: **Petra würde lieber Zivildienst machen, weil sie nicht soviel für das Militär übrig hat.**
Petra would rather do civilian service, because she does not think very highly of military service.

C. **Alles klar**? Answer the following questions in complete sentences.

1. Wer muß in Deutschland zur Bundeswehr oder Zivildienst machen?
2. Wie lange dauern Militärdienst und Zivildienst?
3. Warum lehnen viele junge Leute den Militärdienst ab?
4. Warum gehen einige junge Leute lieber zum Bund?
5. Gibt es in USA auch eine Militärpflicht (draft)?

D. **FÜR ZWEI**

Wie würden Sie sich entscheiden? Würden Sie lieber zum Bund gehen oder Zivildienst machen? Sprechen Sie mit Ihrem/Ihrer Partner/in über Ihre Entscheidung.

Ich bin der Meinung, / finde, / glaube, daß...

wir die/keine Wehrpflicht (draft) brauchen.
Frauen auch (nicht) zum Bund gehen sollten.
man das Geld für andere Zwecke benützen könnte.

Begründen Sie Ihre Meinung:

Ich finde das auch, / bin dagegen, / bin auch dagegen, / bin anderer Meinung, weil...

wir mehr Soldaten brauchen.
ich Krieg und Gewalt nicht gut finde.
Frauen nichts vom Militär verstehen.
andere Länder auch eine Wehrpflicht haben.
die Soldatenausbildung sehr hart ist.

Scene 2: Interviews with Young Bundeswehr Soldiers in Training

chapter 3 to 4

der Appell,-e roll call
Ausbildungsblock,-̈e educational unit, exercise
Bergmarsch,-̈e mountain marching
Dienst duty, service
Drill,-s drill
Marsch,-̈e marching
Nachmittags-Ausblock afternoon duty
Schluß,-̈sse end of duty
Urlaub vacation
Zusammenhalt team spirit

die Ausrüstung,-en equipment, outfit
Division,-en division
Fitness fitness
Gebirgsdivision,-en special mountaineer division
Kameradschaft camaraderie
Kaserne,-n barrack
Lust (auf) interest (in)

das Abenteuer,- adventure
Erlebnis,-se experience
Gebirge,- mountain chain
Reinigen cleaning
Wecken waking call

beschreiben to describe
sich melden to report, register

abenteuerlich adventurous
drillmäßig drill-like
es geht an die Arbeit work begins
mit Sicherheit certainly, definitely
sich zum Appell melden to report for duty
verloren lost
Was hat dir das gebracht? What did you benefit from this?
dagegen on the contrary
einmal here: for once
langatmig longwinded, boring

E. <u>Alles klar</u>? Fill in the blanks as you watch the episode.

Sonja: Sehr viele junge Männer entscheiden sich für die Bundeswehr. Heute bin ich zu Gast bei der ersten Gebirgsdivision in Mittenwald, wo junge Soldaten ausgebildet werden.

Many young men decide in favor of the military service. Today I am a guest of the first mountaineer division in Mittenwald, where young soldiers are being trained.

Sonja: Warum bist du zur Bundeswehr gegangen?

Hartmut: Ich bin eigentlich aus reiner Abenteuerlust zur ____________ gegangen.
Sonja: Macht dir die Ausbildung Spaß?

Hartmut: Also, ich hab's mir etwas __________________ vorgestellt und nicht ganz so drillmäßig.

Sonja: Macht dir die Ausbildung Spaß?
Lutz: Die Bergausbildung macht besonders viel ______, dagegen die Waffen-

ausbildung, die etwas langatmig ist, ______________.
Sonja: Wie lange bist du denn schon hier?

Lutz: Ein Jahr und einen _______.
Sonja: Wie lange mußt du noch?

Lutz: ______ Tage.
Sonja: Müßt ihr immerzu in der Kaserne bleiben?
Lutz: Nein, ab 17 Uhr haben wir Dienstschluß, da ________ wir bis zum Wecken raus.
Sonja: Beschreib bitte mal einen typischen Tag hier!

Raul: Der Tag fängt an mit 6 Uhr ____________, dann erst mal frühstücken, danach meistens irgendein Ausbildungsblock, manchmal auch Bergmärsche,

dann ______________, danach Nachmittags-Ausblock, oder, wenn man vom

Bergmarsch zurückkommt, Reinigen der Ausrüstung, _________________, danach Dienstschluß.

Sonja: Nach dem Frühstück melden sich die Soldaten zum Dienstappell. Danach geht's an die Arbeit.

Sonja: Warum bist du zum Bund gegangen?
Norbert: Bei uns im Dorf ist es allgemein so, daß eigentlich keiner ________________ macht, sondern jeder einfach zum Bund geht.
Sonja: Findest du, Mädchen sollen auch zum Bund?
Detlev: Nein, finde ich nicht, weil die Ausbildung ist doch manchmal etwas _______

und da würde manches Mädchen mit Sicherheit _________________ haben.

Sonja: Wieviel Urlaub hat man in den 15 Monaten?

Dieter: ______ Tage, ist hart, zu wenig.
Sonja: Was hat dir diese Zeit persönlich gebracht?

Dieter: Einmal die Kameradschaft, körperliche ______________, Zusammenhalt in

der Gruppe und natürlich das Erlebnis an der Natur, hier in den __________.
Sonja: Findest du, daß die Zeit beim Bund ein verlorenes Jahr ist?
Ekkehard: Nein, das würd' ich nicht sagen, denn man hat viel Spaß bei der __________, nur Geld verdient man halt keins.

F. **Welche Vorteile** (advantages) **und welche Nachteile** (disadvantages) **hat die Ausbildung bei der Bundeswehr? Machen Sie eine Liste!**

Vorteile	**Nachteile**

G. **FÜR ZWEI: Tagesablauf**

a) Find out about your partner's daily routine:

- When does he/she get up?
- What does he/she do in the morning, in the afternoon, in the evening?
- When does he/she work? What does your partner do with free time?
- When does he/she go to bed?

b) If you were in the army, what would be different in your daily routine? Compare your life now to life as a soldier. For example: "I could not sleep till ten every morning, I would get up at six..."

"Soldat oder Zivi?"

Scene 3: Interview with Klaus Keller, in Civilian Service

chapter 4 to 5

der Erzieher,- educator
Geruch,¨-e smell
Kaufmann,¨-er merchant
Morgenkreis,-e morning circle
Therapeut,-en therapist

die Aufgabe,-n task, duty
Betriebswirtschaft business administration
Behinderung,-en handicap
Bewegung,-en movement, exercise
Doppelbehinderung,-en double handicap
Tätigkeit,-en activity
Wasserratte,-n person who loves to be in the water
Mahlzeit,-en meal

das Geräusch,-e sound, noise
Heim,-e home, institution

aus/führen (führt aus) to carry out
beruhigen to appease, calm down
etwas vor/bereiten (bereitet vor) to prepare something
füttern to feed
schreien to scream, cry
sich entschließen (entschlossen) to decide
verbringen (mit) to spend (with)

behindert impaired, handicapped
blind blind
geduldig patient
geistig mental
körperlich physical
pflegerisch nursing
schwerbehindert severely handicapped
selbständig independent
sensibel sensitive
überwiegend mostly
zur Zeit at this time

Sonja: Nun werdet ihr Klaus Keller kennenlernen, der vor kurzem seine Entscheidung getroffen hat. Er hat sich entschlossen, Zivi, d.h. Zivildienstleistender zu werden, und er arbeitet mit behinderten Kindern.
Now you will meet Klaus Keller, who made up his mind recently. He decided to become a Zivi, that means a civilian servant, and he is working with disabled children.

Klaus: Mein Name ist Klaus Keller. Ich bin 27 Jahre alt. Im Moment mache ich meinen Zivildienst in einem Heim für schwerbehinderte Kinder. Jeden Tag verbringe ich hier 8 Stunden mit den Kindern.

Sonja: Alex kann nicht alleine stehen, aber er liebt Bewegung. Im Heim wohnen zur Zeit 97 blinde und behinderte Kinder. Außer den Erziehern und Therapeuten arbeiten hier 25 Zivis. Franz Martin ist 5 Jahre alt und eine richtige Wasserratte. Alle Kinder fühlen sich im Wasser sehr wohl.

Was für eine Art Zivildienst machst du?

Klaus: Ich arbeite hier mit schwerstbehinderten Kindern. Sie haben alle eine Doppelbehinderung, sind blind als auch geistig behindert als auch körperlich behindert, und es sind überwiegend pflegerische Arbeiten, die ich hier ausführe.

Sonja: Wie lange machst du das schon?

Klaus: Ich mach' es seit Oktober letzten Jahres und werde es bis Mai nächsten Jahres machen.

Sonja: Der Tag beginnt mit dem Aufwecken.

Klaus: Alex kann nicht gehen, deshalb trage ich ihn. Alex ist der Älteste hier, er ist 21 Jahre alt. Auch beim Zähneputzen muß ich helfen.

Sonja: Klaus, was für eine Ausbildung brauchst du, um hier zu arbeiten?

Klaus: Keine Ausbildung, ich lern' hier alles, wenn ich anfange.

Sonja: Und, welche besonderen Eigenschaften braucht man, um mit behinderten Kindern zu arbeiten?

Klaus: Man muß geduldig sein, würd' ich sagen, und die Kinder verstehen, versuchen zu verstehen. Jeden Morgen gibt es einen Morgenkreis.

Heute machen wir ein bißchen Musik. Sandra ist 5 Jahre alt. Sie kann nicht sehen und auch nicht sprechen. Aber sie versteht viel. Sie versteht mehr als die meisten anderen Kinder.

Obwohl die Kinder nicht sehen können, genießen sie die verschiedenen Gerüche und Geräusche.

On Screen

Wer aus Gewissensgründen den Kriegsdienst verweigert, kann zum Zivildienst verpflichtet werden. Meistens arbeiten Zivis mit alten, kranken oder behinderten Menschen.
Whoever becomes a conscientious objector can be drafted into the civilian community service. In most cases Zivis work with old, sick or disabled people.

Sonja: Macht dir die Arbeit Spaß?
Klaus: Wie man sieht, ja.
Sonja: Und was hat es dir persönlich gebracht?
Klaus: Ich bin für Kinder sensibler geworden.
Sonja: Was wirst du machen, wenn der Zivildienst zu Ende ist?
Klaus: Ich werde als Kaufmann arbeiten. Ich habe Betriebswirtschaft studiert.

Klaus: Eine meiner Aufgaben ist, bei den Mahlzeiten zu helfen. Hier bereite ich gerade Essen vor. Das Essen ist hier sehr gesund und frisch. Das ist besonders wichtig für diese Kinder.

Klaus: Die Kinder wohnen in einer Kleingruppe zusammen, wie eine Familie.
Sie können nicht selbständig essen—deshalb muß ich sie füttern.
Carmen ist die schwierigste der Kinder. Sie schreit oft und ist aggressiv gegen sich selbst. Sie kann als einzige der Kinder sehen und laufen. Carmen liebt Musik.
Das beruhigt sie sofort.

H. **Alles klar?** Choose the correct answers as you watch the video.

1. Klaus Keller ist

   a) Zivi b) Erzieher c) Therapeut

2. Klaus ist

   a) 72 b) 17 c) 27

3. Außer Klaus arbeiten im Heim noch

   a) 97 Therapeuten b) 25 Zivis c) 27 Erzieher

4. Klaus arbeitet

   a) mit blinden Erziehern
   b) mit behinderten Kindern
   c) mit geistig behinderten Zivis

5. Um mit behinderten Kindern zu arbeiten, muß man

   a) geduldig sein
   b) eine Ausbildung haben
   c) 21 Jahre alt sein

6. Die Kinder können nicht

   a) riechen b) hören c) sehen

I. Now watch the video for a second time and describe the children Klaus works with. Make a list while watching the movie and write complete sentences later. (At least one sentence per child).

Alex:________________________________

____

Franz Martin:____________________________

Sandra:________________________________

Carmen:_______________________________

____

J. **Alles klar? Beantworten Sie folgende Fragen! Schreiben Sie die Antwort auf!**

1. Wozu hat sich Klaus Keller vor kurzem entschlossen?
2. Wie verbringt Klaus seinen Tag?
3. Beschreiben Sie die Arbeit von Klaus. (mindestens 5 Sätze)
4. Was hat die Arbeit Klaus persönlich gebracht?
5. Welche Pläne hat Klaus für seine Zukunft?

"Soldat oder Zivi"

K. FÜR ZWEI

Vergleichen Sie die Arbeit der Soldaten bei der ersten Gebirgsdivision und die Arbeit von Klaus.

Was wären Sie lieber, Soldat oder Zivi? Sprechen Sie mit Ihrem/Ihrer Partner/in über diese Frage.

Beispiel: Ich wäre lieber Zivi, weil die Arbeit mit Kranken mir mehr bringen würde.

Ich wäre lieber Soldat, / Zivi, weil....

die körperliche Fitness	mir mehr bringen würde.
die Arbeit mit Kindern	mir mehr Spaß machen würde.
die Arbeit mit Kranken	
die Kameradschaft	mir nichts bringen würde.
das frühe Aufstehen	keinen Spaß machen würde.
die Waffenausbildung	?
?	

PROGRAMM 20

SERVUS BAYERN!

On this farewell trip through Bavaria, Sonja takes us to some of the most popular Bavarian tourist attractions, such as the Bavarian lakes, a famous castle and a costume festival. We meet tourists from all walks of life and learn from some of the natives about their traditions.

Schloß Neuschwanstein

LANGUAGE FUNCTIONS

- expressing personal wishes and intentions
- talking about dream vacations

CONTENTS

- sightseeing in Bavaria
- contrary-to-fact statements
- customs and regional characteristics
- stereotypes
- review

chapter 5 to 13

Scene 1: Talking to Vacationers in Bavaria

der **Großstadttrubel** big city stress
See,-n lake
Starnberger See Bavarian lake near the town of Starnberg
Trubel commotion

die **Erholung,-en** relaxation, rest
Pfingstferien (plural) vacation at Whitsun

das **Babysitten** babysitting

Leipzig big city in Saxony

sich erholen (von) to relax (from), to recover (from)

locker easy going, relaxed
zur Erholung to relax

A. Alles klar? Make a list.

Woher kommen die Leute?	**Was machen sie hier?**
______________________	______________________
______________________	______________________
______________________	______________________
______________________	______________________

Sonja: Woher kommen Sie?
Man: Ich komme aus Limburg.
Sonja: Machen Sie hier Urlaub?
Man: Ja, über die Pfingstferien.
Sonja: Mit wem sind Sie hier?
Man: Mit meiner Freundin.
Sonja: Was wollen Sie hier machen?
Woman: Wir wollen mal nach München fahren und halt hier baden.
Sonja: Wie finden Sie Bayern?
Woman: Sehr schön; die Leute sind hier viel lockerer wie bei uns zuhause.

Sonja: Woher kommen Sie?
Woman: Wir kommen aus München.
Sonja: Und mit wem sind Sie hier?
Woman: Mit der Familie, mit meinem Mann, mit den Verwandten aus Leipzig und mit meinen Kindern.

Sonja: Für wie lange sind Sie hier?
Woman: Für heute nachmittag zum Baden.
Sonja: Kommen Sie jeden Tag hierher?
Man 2: Nein, ich bin hier so zwei-, dreimal in der Woche, so zur Erholung.
Sonja: Und was machen Sie hier?
Man 2: Heute bin ich nur zum Baden und zum Babysitten, aber sonst geh' ich windsurfen, schwimmen, vielleicht manchmal segeln, Wasserski fahren.

Sonja: Diesen Sommer verbringe ich mit Freunden.

B. **Alles klar? Schreiben Sie die Antwort!**

1. Wo ist Sonja jetzt?

2. Warum ist Sonja dort?

3. Welche Urlaubspläne hat Sonja diesen Sommer?

C. **FÜR ZWEI**

Welche Urlaubspläne haben Sie diesen Sommer? Sprechen Sie mit Ihrem/Ihrer Partner/in über Ihre Urlaubspläne! (Wohin? Mit wem? Wie lange? Warum?)

chapter 7 to 8

Scene 2: Interviews with Rowers

der **Ruderer,-** rower

die **Kraft,¨-e** strength, power

faulenzen to be lazy, idle
rudern to row

anstrengend hard, tiresome **ungemütlich** uncomfortable

Sonja: Sportlich ist hier viel los, vor allem auf dem Wasser. Viele Münchner kommen am Wochenende hierher, z.B. zum Rudern.
In terms of sports, there is a lot going on here, especially on the water. Many people from Munich come here on the weekend in order to row, for example.

> *On Screen*
>
> **Der Starnberger See ist in 30 Minuten von München aus zu erreichen. An der tiefsten Stelle ist er über 120 Meter tief.**
> Lake Starnberg is only a half-hour drive away from Munich. At the deepest spot, it is over 120 meters deep.

D. Alles klar? Fill in the blanks as you watch the video.

Sonja: Woher kommst du?

Reinhard: Ich komme aus _______________.
Sonja: Was machst du dieses Wochenende?
Reinhard: Ich werd' rudern und faulenzen.
Sonja: Wie oft gehst du rudern?

Reinhard: Ich geh' dreimal die _______________ rudern.
Sonja: Was gefällt dir am Rudern?
Reinhard: Daß es nicht so anstrengend ist wie andere Sportarten.

Sonja: Seit wann ruderst du schon?
Angela: Ich rudere jetzt seit zwei Jahren.
Sonja: Wie bist du dazu gekommen?

Angela: Durch die _______________.
Sonja: Also — auch Mädchen rudern?

Angela: Ja, aber mehr _______________.
Sonja: Warum machen es nur wenige Mädchen?

Angela: Man braucht viel _______________.
Sonja: Ist es manchmal etwas ungemütlich auf dem Wasser?

Angela: Ja, man muß sich warm _______________.

Sonja: Woher kommst du?

Dirk: Ich komme aus ______________.

Sonja: Was machst du dieses Wochenende?

Dirk: Heute tu' ich rudern und morgen werde ich vielleicht zum ______________ gehen.

Sonja: Wie oft ruderst du in der Woche?

Dirk: Ich ruder' einmal in der Woche, ______________.

Sonja: Und wie hat es mit den Rudern bei dir angefangen?

Dirk: Ich bin durch die ______________ zum Rudern gekommen.

E. **Watch the video a second time and match the person with the correct statement.**

1. **Reinhard** a) findet es oft ungemütlich auf dem Wasser

2. **Dirk** b) rudert seit zwei Jahren

3. **Angela** c) rudert einmal in der Woche

4. **Angela** d) findet rudern nicht so anstrengend wie andere Sportarten

5. **Reinhard** e) geht morgen vielleicht zum Segeln

6. **Dirk** f) geht dieses Wochenende faulenzen

F. **Alles klar? Beantworten Sie folgende Fragen. Bilden Sie vollständige Sätze.**

1. Wo liegt der Starnberger See?
2. Was kann man dort machen?
3. Was gefällt Reinhard am Rudern?
4. Warum rudern mehr Jungen als Mädchen?
5. Wie sind Angela und Dirk zum Rudern gekommen?

Scene 3: Windsurfing

Sonja: Meine Idee von einem perfekten Urlaub ist nicht zu faulenzen, sondern sich aktiv zu betätigen. Ich probiere am liebsten neue Sportarten aus, z.B. Windsurfen.

On Screen

Windsurfen begann 1968 in Kalifornien und ist seit 1984 eine olympische Disziplin.
Windsurfen kann man am besten auf Hawaii, den Fidschi-Inseln und in Kalifornien.
Windsurfing began in 1968 in California and has been an Olympic sport since 1984.
Windsurfing can be done best in Hawaii, the Fiji Islands and in California.

Jens: Wie gefällt's dir denn?
Sonja: Ein bißchen schwierig, aber ganz gut.

Cultural Note

Windsurfing has become very popular in Germany. There are hardly any lakes left that are not dotted by the windsurfers' colorful sails. Since all the German shops and businesses are closed on weekends, lots of Germans use this time to pursue an outdoor activity. With nice weekend weather, people who like to get away from a crowded city frequently find themselves sitting in traffic jams together with other people who have the same idea.

Sonja Windsurfing

Scene 4: Asking What Tourists Think of a Bavarian Castle

chapter 9 to 10

die Ähnlichkeit,-en similarity

das Image,-s image, reputation
Schloß, pl. **Schlösser** castle

enttäuschen to disappoint

ausgestattet decked out
barock baroque
beeindruckend impressive
belgisch Belgian
herrlich splendid
kitschig tacky, kitchy
pompös pompous
sehenswert worth seeing
sympathisch pleasant, nice
überladen overburdened, cluttered

Von diesem Schloß bin ich enttäuscht I am disappointed by this castle.
..es gibt nicht sehr viel zu sehen ...there is not much to see

On Screen

Schloß Linderhof ist eines der Schlösser von König Ludwig II von Bayern. Linderhof wurde 1878 vollendet.
Linderhof Castle is one of King Ludwig II's castles. Linderhof was completed in 1878.

Cultural Note

Ludwig II (1845-1886) became king of Bavaria in 1864. He is famous for his fondness of constructing many fairy-tale like castles such as **Neuschwanstein** and **Herrenchiemsee**. He was also a great admirer and patron of the composer Richard Wagner. In 1886 he became insane. He and his personal physician drowned under mysterious circumstances in Lake Starnberg.

G. <u>Alles klar</u>? Fill in the blanks as you watch the video film.

Sonja: Woher kommen Sie?

Man: Ich komme aus ________________________.
Sonja: Mit wem sind Sie hier?

Man: Wir haben belgische Freunde zu ____________________, und die wollen Bayern ________________________, und darum sind wir heute hier.
Sonja: Wie finden Sie das Schloß?

Man: Für mich ist es zu ____________________ und zu barock, aber ich glaube, daß es gut zu dem Image von Ludwig dem Zweiten __________________.
Sonja: Wie finden Sie das Schloß?

Woman: Sympathisch, romantisch, einfach ____________________.

Sonja: Und wie finden Sie dieses Schloß?
Man: Das Schloß find' ich sehr romantisch, sehr __________________ ausgestattet; es hat viel Ähnlichkeit mit den ____________________________ Schlössern, mit dem barocken Stil, und für meinen ____________________ etwas zu überladen.

> *Cultural Note*
>
> **Schloß Neuschwanstein wurde 1868-86 erbaut, doch nie fertiggestellt.**
> Neuschwanstein Castle was built from 1868-86 but never completed.

Sonja: Wie findest du dieses Schloß?

Girl: ________________________, ein bißchen pompös, dem Stil des König Ludwig entsprechend.

Sonja: Wie finden Sie das Schloß?
Man: Herrlich, romantisch, ist ___________________________, wunderschön!

Woman: Von diesem Schloß bin ich etwas _______________________; ich stellte es mir größer vor.

Sonja: Wie findest du dieses Schloß?

Woman: Von außen ziemlich _______________________, aber innen nur wenige Zimmer, und es gibt nicht sehr viel zu ____________________ darin.

H. **FÜR ZWEI**

Beantworten Sie folgende Fragen mit Ihrem/Ihrer Partner/in! Proceed according to the example.

Beispiel: A. **Was finden Sie ungemütlich?**
B. **Die Stühle im Klassenzimmer finde ich ungemütlich.**
A. **Das ist ein ungemütliches Klassenzimmer.**

1. Was finden Sie kitschig?
2. Wen finden Sie sympathisch?
3. Wen oder was finden Sie pompös?
4. Was ist barock?
5. Was ist sehenswert?
6. Was ist beeindruckend?
7. Was ist romantisch?
8. Wovon sind Sie enttäuscht?

Scene 5: Asking About Dream Vacations

chapter 10 to 11

der Dschungel jungle

die Bahamas
Gegend,-en area, region
Karibik Caribbean
Landschaft,-en landscape
Malediven (plural) Maldives (Maldive Islands)
Palme,-n palm tree
Weltreise,-n trip around the world
Wüste,-n desert

Amerika America (people generally mean the U.S.)
Australien Australia

durch/gehen (geht durch) to go through

Lanzarote one of the Canary Islands

Neuseeland New Zealand

exotisch exotic

es schaut kein Mensch nobody looks you over
jemand blöd anquatschen (slang) to address someone in an unfriendly manner

Remember:	**Ich würde gern...** I would like to...
	Ich wäre gern... I would like to be...

Sonja: Mir gefällt's hier in Bayern, aber ich würde auch gern in exotischere Gegenden fahren, z.B. auf die Malediven oder die Bahamas. Ich fragte Leute: Was wäre dein Traumurlaub?

Georg: Ja, wir vier haben unseren Traumurlaub schon—wir fliegen im Sommer nach Lanzarote.

I. **Alles klar? Was sagen die anderen? Was wäre ihr Traumurlaub?** (take notes)

Marco: ______________________________

Heike: ______________________________

Klaus: ______________________________

Verena: ______________________________

Vanessa: ______________________________

Karsten: ______________________________

Jens: ______________________________

Monika: ______________________________

Petra: ______________________________

Bernd: ______________________________

Monika sagt: Eine Weltreise, möglichst lang.
Monika says: A trip around the world, as long as possible.

J. **Wie sagt man?**

1. as old as possible ______________________________
2. as short as possible ______________________________
3. as romantic as possible ______________________________
4. as cheap as possible ______________________________

> In adjectival position (in front of a noun), the adjective following **möglichst** takes the appropriate adjective ending.
>
> **Zum Beispiel:** Ich würde eine möglichst lang**e** Weltreise machen.
> Nach Alaska würde ich einen möglichst warm**en** Anorak mitnehmen.

K. **FÜR ZWEI**

Let's assume you are going on a trip to Europe next summer.

Beispiel:
A. Mit wem würdest du reisen?
B. Ich würde mit ein**em** möglichst reich**en** Mann reisen.

Use the example as a model to work with a partner.

1. Was für Kleidung würdest du mitnehmen?
2. Wo würdest du übernachten?
3. Wen würdest du mitnehmen?
4. Was würdest du mitbringen?
5. Wie würdest du reisen?
6. Wo würdest du essen?

L. **FÜR ZWEI**

Wie stellen Sie sich Ihren Traumurlaub vor? Sprechen Sie mit Ihrem/Ihrer Partner/in über Ihren Traumurlaub.

Beispiel: **Wohin würden Sie fliegen? Ich würde nach Spanien fliegen,** etc.

		fliegen		
Wohin		fahren		
Mit wem		gehen		
Wo	**würden Sie**	übernachten	?	**Ich würde......**
		essen		
Was		machen		
		mitnehmen		
Wie		reisen		
Wie lange		bleiben		

chapter 11 to 12

Scene 6: At a "Trachtenfest," a Bavarian Costume Festival

der **Anlaß,¨-sse** occasion
Brauch,¨-e custom
Einwohner,- inhabitant
Festzug,¨-e parade
Gottesdienst,-e church service
Verein,-e club, organization

die **Feier,-n** celebration
Gemeinde,-n community
Hochzeit,-en wedding
Tracht,-en traditional ethnic costume

das **Aussehen** physical appearance
Fest,-e celebration, feast
Erscheinungsbild,-er image

bevorzugen to prefer
kirchlich related to the church
umgeben surrounding
verschönern to beautify, make more attractive

zu den entsprechenden Anlässen on the appropriate occasions

Cultural Note

Some of the people interviewed in this video speak standard high German with a Bavarian accent. They do not speak dialect, which would mean that not only their pronunciation, but also their grammar and vocabulary, would differ from the standard high German. The word **mei** is only used in Bavaria. It is a particle which introduces a new sentence and means something like the English "well," as in "Well, how are you?"

On Screen

Bayern ist sehr traditionsbewußt und konservativ. Die katholische Kirche spielt hier eine wichtige Rolle. Heute schau' ich mir in Egling das Trachtenfest an.
Bavaria is very conscious of its traditions and is conservative. The Catholic church plays a big role. Today I am going to watch the costume festival in Egling.

Sonja: Die Einwohner aus den umliegenden Gemeinden treffen sich heute zu einem großen Festzug. Danach werden sie zu einem Gottesdienst gehen. Heute trägt hier jeder Tracht—auch die ganz kleinen.

Sonja: Wann tragen Sie Tracht?
Woman: Am Sonntag oder bei Festen.
Sonja: Wann tragen Sie Tracht?
Man: Sonntags, feiertags.
Sonja: Und wieso?
Man: Mei, das ist bei uns der Brauch.
Sonja: Wann tragen Sie Tracht?
Woman: Wann? Zu solchen Anlässen wie hier.
Sonja: Und warum?
Woman: Das Erscheinungsbild vom Verein wird damit einfach verschönert, und wir wollen halt dazu beitragen.

Sonja: Trägt jeder Tracht?
Woman 2: Die hier mitgehen schon, ja.

Sonja: Wann tragen Sie Tracht?
Man: Jeden Tag.
Sonja: Und warum?
Man: Weil das bei uns so der Brauch ist.
Sonja: Trägt jeder Tracht?
Man: Jeder, der eine hat.

Sonja: Würdest du Tracht tragen?
Jochen: Ich würde, zu den entsprechenden Anlässen würde ich immer eine Tracht bevorzugen.
Sonja: Welche Anlässe sind das?
Jochen: Eine Hochzeit, eine große Feier in Bayern, eine kirchliche Feier.
Sonja: Würdest du Tracht tragen?
Annette: Nein.
Sonja: Warum nicht?
Annette: Das paßt irgendwie zu meinem, zu meinem Aussehen irgendwie paßt das nicht, auch zu meiner Sprache—ich sprech' nicht Bayrisch.

Sonja: Trägst du manchmal Tracht?
Oskar: Nein, eigentlich nie.
Sonja: Warum nicht?
Oskar: Ist mir zu konservativ, und es paßt eigentlich auch nicht zu mir.

Sonja: Trägst du manchmal Tracht?
Shamin: Nein, überhaupt nicht.

Cultural Note

Trachten (traditional costumes) are worn only in the southernmost part of Bavaria. Because of their spectacular appearance, these costumes have attracted the attention of foreigners and become stereotypical. The significance of these outfits should not be overstated. Only a small percentage of the German population owns a **Tracht**. Although people in many parts of rural Germany have their own traditional costumes, these are generally worn only for very special occasions such as historical celebrations or cultural festivities. In most parts of Germany except for the alpine regions, people generally do not wear traditional outfits.

M. **Fragen zum Video**. There are several answers to each question. List them all.

1. **Wann und bei welchen Anlässen tragen "die Bayern" eine Tracht?**

a. ______________________ b. ______________________

c. ______________________ d. ______________________

e. ______________________ f. ______________________

2. **Warum tragen die Leute eine Tracht?**

a. ______________________________

b. ______________________________

3. **Warum tragen Anette und Oskar keine Tracht?**

Anette:______________________________

Oskar:______________________________

4. **Welche Leute tragen keine Tracht? Was ist Ihre Meinung?**

____

____

5. **Tragen viele Deutsche eine Tracht? Was ist Ihre Meinung?**

____

____

N. **FÜR ZWEI ODER MEHERE: Urlaub in Bayern**

Imagine you are working for a travel agency and have to write a description for a brochure about Bavaria. Make it sound so interesting that your customers will want to go there.

- What is there to do and to see?
- What is special about the place?

Talk about landscape, sights, mentality of the people, history, local customs, food, climate and accommodations. Discuss with your partner(s) what should be in the brochure and then write the description together.

O. **FÜR ZWEI**

Würden Sie eine Tracht tragen, wenn Sie in Bayern wohnen würden? Sprechen Sie mit Ihrem/Ihrer Partner/in darüber.

P. **Grammar Review (Perfect Tense). Haben oder Sein?**

1. Letzten Sommer ____________________ wir in Bayern gewesen.
2. Wir ____________________ immer in der Jugendherberge übernachtet.
3. Wie ____________________ Ihnen das Essen geschmeckt?
4. Gut. Wir ____________________ immer bei McDonalds gegessen.
5. Wir ____________________ im Starnberger See gebadet.
6. ____________________ Sie das Schloß Linderhof gesehen?
7. Hoffentlich ____________________ Sie ein bißchen Deutsch gelernt.
8. Nein, leider nicht, die Leute ____________________ entweder Bayrisch oder Englisch gesprochen.
9. ____________________ Sie auch München besucht?
10. In München ____________________ wir oft in den Biergarten gegangen.

chapter 12 to 13

Scene 7: What Are the Bavarians Like?

der Bayer,-n Bavarian (person)

die Mentalität,-en character

aufgeschlossen open-minded
bierbäuchig with a beer belly
eher rather
erfolgreich successful
gemütlich warm, comfortable to be with
gesellig sociable, gregarious
grantig (slang) irritable, unfriendly
grob uncouth, coarse
humorvoll has a sense of humor
mürrisch morose
plump plump
stolz proud

sich unterscheiden von to differ from
alles Gute! all the best!
eine Prüfung bestehen to pass an exam

Sonja: Die Leute haben sich zu einem feierlichen Gottesdienst im Freien versammelt.

On Screen

In Bayern leben fast elf Millionen Menschen, davon sind ungefähr 70% katholisch, 26% evangelisch und 1% Mohammedaner.
Almost eleven million people live in Bavaria. About 70% are Catholic, 26% Protestant and 1% Muslim.

Sonja: Wie würden Sie den typischen Bayern beschreiben?
Man: Wenn es einen gibt, dann ist er eher gemütlich, etwas langsamer, mag gerne Bier, ist nicht hektisch.
Sonja: Sind Sie selbst stolz, Bayer zu sein?
Man: Ja, bin ich schon.

Q. Alles klar?

1. Wie würden Sie die typischen Eigenschaften der Bayern beschreiben? Make a list as you watch the video.

______________	______________	______________
______________	______________	______________
______________	______________	______________

2. Wie unterscheiden sich die Bayern von den anderen Deutschen?

3. Warum sind die Bayern stolz, Bayern zu sein?

4. Sind Sie stolz, Amerikaner zu sein?

Tracht

Q. **FÜR ZWEI**

Klischees, Klischees! Diskutieren Sie mit Ihrem/Ihrer Partner/in die kulturellen Unterschiede! Vergleichen Sie die typischen Amerikaner mit den typischen Deutschen!

R. **FÜR EINE/N, ZWEI ODER MEHRERE: Bayrisches Alphabet**

A wie Alpen
B wie BMW
C wie Chiemsee

Find a thing, a name, or an idea related to Bavaria for each letter of the alphabet! (or as many as you can!)

S. **Video Magazin**

Erinnern Sie sich? In this comprehensive review of **Lernexpreß II** you may test your memory!

1. **Was hat Sonja in Garmisch-Partenkirchen gemacht?**

   a) Windsurfen   b) Skilaufen   c) Tae-Kwon-Do

2. **Was ist Kaiserschmarren?**

   a) eine Stadt in Bayern   b) ein Hotel in München   c) eine Mehlspeise

3. **Wo fanden 1936 die Olympischen Winterspiele statt?**

   a) in München   b) in Garmisch-Partenkirchen   c) in Mittenwald

4. **Wo ist das Deutsche Museum?**

   a) in München b) in Garmisch-Partenkirchen c) in Mittenwald

5. **Was ist der Viktualienmarkt?**

   a) ein Gemüsemarkt b) ein großer Park c) ein Antiquitätenmarkt

6. **Wie heißt der bekannte Münchner Fußballverein?**

   a) Bayrischer Rundfunk b) Borussia München c) Bayern München

7. **Der Englische Garten ist**

   a) ein Park in London b) ein Park in München c) ein Fußballstadion

8. **Tae-Kwon-Do ist**

   a) ein neuer Modetanz b) eine Kampfsportart c) ein chinesisches Nudelgericht

9. **Faustball ist ein Sport, den man**

   a) alleine spielt b) zu zweit spielt c) in einem Team spielt

10. **Müsli ißt man**

    a) morgens b) mittags c) abends

11. **München hat**

    a) 600 000 Einwohner b) 1,2 Millionen Einwohner c) 2 Millionen Einwohner

12. **Leute, die zu dick sind, haben**

    a) Schwergewicht b) Mittelgewicht c) Übergewicht

13. **Deutsche Schüler tragen**

    a) eine Schuluniform b) einen Trainingsanzug c) was sie wollen.

14. **Auf einem Flohmarkt kann man**

    a) Gemüse kaufen b) alte Sachen kaufen c) Autos kaufen

15. **Fasching ist**

    a) im Winter b) im Herbst c) im Sommer

16. **Viele Touristen kommen nach Mittenwald wegen**

    a) der Umweltverschmutzung b) der Berge c) Fasching

17. **An Fasching tragen viele Mittenwalder**

a) Designerklamotten b) Holzmasken c) Kaschmirmäntel

18. **Der Film "Das Boot" wurde**

a) 1961 gedreht b) 1971 gedreht c) 1981 gedreht

19. **Ein Stuntman muß**

a) musikalisch sein b) eine gute Aussprache haben c) sportlich sein

20. **Eine Moderatorin muß**

a) gut reden können b) musikalisch sein c) sich für Technik interessieren

21. **Der Bayrische Rundfunk ist**

a) ein Fernsehprogramm b) eine private Radiostation
c) eine öffentlichrechtliche Radiostation

22. **Die Ausbildung zum Bierbrauer dauert**

a) 5 Jahre b) 7 Jahre c) 3 Jahre

23. **König Ludwig II lebte**

a) im 17. Jahrhundert b) im 18. Jahrhundert c) im 19. Jahrhundert

24. **Die Ausbildungszeit bei der Bundeswehr ist**

a) kürzer als der Zivildienst b) länger als der Zivildienst
c) so lang wie der Zivildienst

25. **Das Barock ist ein Baustil des**

a) 15. Jahrhunderts b) 17. Jahrhunderts c) 19. Jahrhunderts

T. FÜR GRUPPEN: Zusammenfassung

Talk with your partners about **Deutschland und die Deutschen:**

- What did you learn from the series?
- Has **Lernexpreß** changed your opinion in any respect?
- Why do you think that many foreigners want to live in Germany?
- Would you like to live in Germany? Why? Why not?
- What would you say if you had to describe Germany and the Germans in two or three sentences?

"Auf Wiedersehen"

GERMAN–ENGLISH VOCABULARY

Abbreviations:

fem.	feminine	dat.	dative
masc.	masculine	coll.	colloquial
sing.	singular	pp.	past participle
pl.	plural		

Plural of Nouns:

The plural of nouns is indicated by what follows the comma after the noun. For example: **der Apparat,-e** has a plural **die Apparate**; **die Addresse,-n** has a plural **die Addressen**. If only a hyphen follows, the plural is the same as the singular: **das Abenteuer,-** has a plural **die Abenteuer**; only the article changes. A noun with an internal vowel change (**Umlaut**) in the plural is indicated by a quote mark over the hyphen: for example, the plural of **der Anzug,¨-e** is **die Anzüge.**

Verbs:

(1) Verbs with stem changes in the present tense have the third person singular of the present tense noted in parenthesis. For example: **treffen (trifft)**.

(2) Verbs with separable prefixes are indicated by a slash between the prefix and the verb stem, as well as by the third person form in parenthesis. For example: **ab/reisen (reist ab).** The slash is only an indicator; the infinitives are written without the slash: **abnehmen, anreisen.**

This is a basic vocabulary for the use of this text. Students are encouraged to purchase one of the inexpensive paperback dictionaries.

A

ab und zu now and then
das Abendbrot = Abendessen supper
das Abenteuer,- adventure
abenteuerlich adventurous
ab/lehnen (lehnt ab) to reject
ab/nehmen (nimmt ab) to lose weight
ab/reisen (reist ab) to leave
abwechslungsreich diverse, varied
die Adresse,-n address
das Aerobics aerobics
die Ähnlichkeit,-en similarity
der Alkohol alcohol
der Alltag everyday
alltäglich everyday
allzuviel too much
all all
vor allem (v.a.) especially, above all
als as
das Alter,- age
Amerika America (generally, the U.S.)
der Anfang,¨-e beginning
an/fangen (fängt an) to begin
an/fertigen (fertigt an) to make, produce
angestellt employed
der Angriffsfußball offensive soccer (aggressive style)
die Angst,¨-e fear
  Angst haben to be afraid
ängstlich frightened, scared
an/haben (hat an) to wear
an etwas kommen to get something
  Wie bist du an deinen Job gekommen? How did you get your job?
der Anlaß,¨-sse occasion
zu den entsprechenden Anlässen on the appropriate occasions
an/probieren (probiert an) to try on
an/schauen (schaut an) to see, here: to visit
anschließend afterwards
an/sehen (sieht an) to look at
  etwas an/sehen to look at or watch something
an/sprechen (spricht an) to speak to, address
  ...wurde mal angesprochen I was once asked
die Anstellung,-en = Stelle,-n job, position
anstrengend hard, tiresome
an/ziehen (zieht an, ist angezogen) to put on; to wear
der Anzug,¨-e suit
die Apfeltasche,-n apple fritter
der Apparat,-e apparatus, contraption
der Appell,-e roll call
  sich zum Appell melden to report for duty
der Appetit appetite
die Arbeit,-en work
  es geht an die Arbeit work begins
die Arbeitszeit,-en hours at work
der Arzt,¨-e physician (masc.)
die Ärztin,-nen physician (fem.)
der Astronaut,-en astronaut (masc.)
die Astronautin,-nen astronaut (fem.)
die Atomkraft nuclear power
auch also
Auf geht's! Let's go!
der Aufbau organization
das Auffassungsvermögen perception
die Aufgabe,-n task, duty
aufgeschlossen open-minded
auf/nehmen (nimmt auf) to absorb
auf/passen (paßt auf) to pay attention
der Aufschnitt,-e assortment of sliced meat and sausage
auf/wachsen (wächst auf) to grow up
aufwendig lavish, costly
aus from, out
  aus dem Ausland from abroad
aus/bilden (bildet aus; ausgebildet) to educate
die Ausbildung,-en education, professional training
der Ausbildungsblock,¨-e educational unit, exercise
(sich etwas) ausdenken (denkt sich etwas aus) to think up something
der Ausflug,¨-e excursion
aus/führen (führt aus) to carry out
aus/geben (gibt aus) to spend
ausgefallen peculiar, exceptional
ausgestattet decked out
ausgezeichnet excellent
aus/kommen (kommt aus) to make do, to cope

ins Ausland abroad
ausländisch foreign
aus/mustern (mustert aus) to discharge from service
aus/packen (packt aus) to unpack
aus/probieren (probiert aus) to try out
die Ausrüstung,-en equipment, outfit
das Aussehen physical appearance
die Aussprache,-n pronunciation
aus/tragen (trägt aus) to carry out
Australien Australia
die Auswahl,-en (an) + dat. choice
der Außendienst service call
außerdem besides, on top of that
die Autolackiererei,-en auto paint shop
der Automobilmechaniker,- car mechanic
der Autoverkehr traffic
der Azubi,-s short for **Auszubildende** apprentice

B

das Babysitten babysitting
der Bäcker,- baker
die Bahamas the Bahamas
die Bank,-en bank
barock baroque
das Baseball sport of baseball
der Baseballhandschuh,-e baseball glove
der Baseballschläger,- baseball bat
der Bauer,-n farmer (m.)
die Bäuerin,-nen farmer (fem.)
der Bayer,-n Bavarian (person)
bayrisch Bavarian
der Bayrische Rundfunk Bavarian public radio
bedienen to operate
beeindruckend impressive
behalten (behält) to keep
behindert impaired, handicapped
die Behinderung,-en handicap
die Belastung,-en burden, stress, pollution
belgisch Belgian
bemalt painted in color
benützen to use
der Bereich,-e field, area
der Berg,-e mountain
der Bergmarsch,¨-e mountain marching
bergsteigen mountain climbing
die Bermudahose,-n Bermuda shorts
der Beruf,-e profession, vocation
beruflich professional
die Berufsschule,-n vocational school
beruhigen to appease, calm down
berühmt famous
sich beschäftigen mit to be occupied with
beschreiben to describe
besonders especially
bestellen to order
bestimmt certain
betreiben = treiben to do
betreuen to advise
der Betrieb,-e company
die Betriebswirtschaft business administration
das Bett,-en bed
die Bevölkerung population
die Bevölkerungsschicht,-en segment of population
bevorzugen to prefer
beweglich flexible
die Bewegung,-en movement, exercise
bewußt conscious, aware
das Bier,-e beer
bierbäuchig with a beer belly
die Bierbrauerei,-en brewery
das Bild,-er picture
der Bildmischer,- video mixer
der Bildspeicher,- picture storage unit
billig cheap
ein bißchen a little
Bitte schön! Here you are!
Bitte schön? What can I do for you?
bleiben to stay
blind blind
die Bluse,-n blouse
das Boot,-e boot
der Brauch,¨-e custom
der Brauer,- brewer
breit wide
bringen to bring
das Brötchen,- roll
die Brutalität violence
der Bund Bundeswehr (abbrev.)
die Bundesliga national major league

das Bundesligaspiel,-e game in national league
die Bundeswehr German army
die Bundeswehr machen (coll.) to join the military service
die Butter,- butter

C

der Cheeseburger,- cheeseburger
die Chemikalie,-n chemical
chemisch chemical
chic = schick elegant, fancy
die Chips here: french fries
der Clown,-s clown
das Computerspiel,-e computer game
die Cutterin,-nen film editor (fem.)

D

dabei sein to participate
dagegen on the contrary
danach after that
dauern to last
dauernd all the time
denken an to think about
das Design,-s design
die Designerin,-nen designer
die Designerklamotten designer clothes (coll.)
die Designermode designer fashions
der Deutsche Meister national champion
die Diät,-en diet
  eine Diät machen to be on a diet
dick fat, obese (people)
der Dienst duty, service
differieren to vary
die Division,-en division
doch however, yet
die Doppelbehinderung,-en double handicap
einen Film drehen to shoot a film
dreieinhalb three-and-a-half
der Drill drill
drillmäßig drill-like
der Dschungel jungle
durch/gehen (geht durch) to go through
dürr skinny

E

egal all the same
eher rather
ehrlich honest
die Eigenschaft,-en quality, characteristic
eigentlich actually
  eigentlich schon/nicht actually yes/not
ein/atmen (atmet ein) to breathe in, absorb
der Eindruck,¨-e impression
einen Eindruck vermitteln to give an impression
einheitlich here: the same
einige some
ein/lernen (lernt ein) to train on the job
einmal once, for once
  einmal am Tag once a day
einmalig excellent
ein/treffen (trifft ein) to arrive
der Einwohner,- inhabitant
das Eis ice cream
das Eishockey ice hockey
das Eiskunstlaufen ice skating
Eisstock schießen curling
die Elektrotechnik electronics
die Energieverschwendung waste of energy
der Englische Garten large park in Munich
entdecken to discover
sich entscheiden to decide
die Entscheidung,-en decision
  eine Entscheidung treffen to make a decision
sich entschließen (entschlossen) to decide
sich entspannen to relax
enttäuschen to disappoint
entwerfen to design
die Erdbeere,-n strawberry
die Erfahrung,-en experience
erfolgreich successful
das Erfolgserlebnis,-se accomplishment
sich ergeben to result
  es hat sich so ergeben it turned out that way
sich erholen (von) to relax (from), to recover (from)

die Erholung,-en relaxation,rest
zur Erholung to relax
sich erinnern (an) + acc. to remember
erleben to experience
das Erlebnis,-se experience
sich ernähren to eat
ernst serious
erreichen to reach
das Erscheinungsbild,-er image
erst only
als erstes at first
erst mal first
der Erzieher,- trainer
exotisch exotic

F

das Fach,¨-er subject, field
die Fachhochschule,-n four-year college
die Fähigkeit,-en ability
fallen (fällt) pp. **gefallen** to fall down
Fallschirm springen parachuting
Fall,¨-e case
auf jeden Fall anyway, anyhow
der Fan,-s fan
fantastisch marvellous
der Fotograf,-en photographer
die Fotografie,-n photography
fotografieren to take pictures
die Fotografin,-nen photographer
das Fotomodell,-e model
farbenfroh colorful
der Fasching carnival, Mardi gras
der Faschingsball,¨-e Mardi gras party
das Faschingskostüm,-e Fasching costume
faulenzen to be lazy, idle
die Faust,¨-e fist
der Faustball,¨-e fistball
die Feier,-n celebration
feiern to celebrate
fern/schauen = fern/sehen to watch TV
der Fernseher,- TV set
das Fernsehprogramm,-e TV channel
das Fernsehpublikum TV audience
fertig finished
das Fest,-e party, celebration
der Festzug,¨-e parade
fett greasy, fat (food)
das Fett,-e fat
der Film,-e film
die Filmbranche,-n film industry
die Filmrolle,-n part in a film
das Filmstudio,-s
die Filmtourführerin,-nen film tour leader (fem.)
der Film,-e film, movie
einen Film drehen to shoot a movie
die Fingerfertigkeit,-en manual dexterity
die Fitness fitness
das Fleckerlgewand,¨-er traditional carnival costume
das Fleisch meat
der Flohmarkt,¨-e flea market
die Folge,-n episode
frei free, unoccupied
im Freien outdoors
die Freizeit,-en free time
sich freuen auf + acc. to look forward to
der Freund,-e friend
freundlich friendly
frisch fresh
die Friseuse,-n hair dresser (fem.)
der Fruchtsaft,¨-e fruit juice
fühlen to feel
sich zuhause fühlen to feel at home
führen to lead
die Führerin,-nen leader (fem.)
die Fülle abundance, variety
der Fußball soccer
füttern to feed

G

gar nicht schlecht not so bad
garniert garnished
der Gast,¨-e customer, guest
zu Gast sein to visit
der Gasthof,¨-e restaurant, inn
gastronomisch gastronomic
das Gebäude,- building
das Gebirge,- mountain chain
die Gebirgsdivision,-en mountain division
der Geburtstag,-e birthday

geduldig patient
gefährlich dangerous
die Gegend,-en area, region
das Gegenteil,-e opposite
  im Gegenteil on the contrary
gehen to go
  es geht nicht so hektisch zu life isn't so stressful
  Es geht schon It's all right
der Geigenbau violin making
die Geigenbauschule,-n violin-making school
der Geist spirit
geistig mental
das Gelände,- terrain, ground, area
gelegentlich occasionally
die Gemeinde,-n community
gemeinsam together
gemischt mixed
das Gemüse (sing.) vegetables
gemütlich cozy, informal
genau wie ich just like me
genießen to enjoy
genug enough
gerade right now
das Gerät,-e piece of apparatus
das Geräusch,-e sound, noise
geregelt regular, formal
gern haben to like
  hättest du gern...? would you like?
  Ich hätte gern... I would like...
die Gerste barley
der Geruch,¨-e smell
gesamt whole, total
die Gesamtarbeitszeit total time at work
der Gesangsunterricht singing lessons
geschäftlich on business
der Geschäftsmann,¨-er businessman
die Geschäftsreise,-n business trip
der Geschmack taste, liking
  wie's dem Geschmack entspricht to one's taste/liking
gesellig social, gregarious
gesund healthy
die Gewalt violence
das Gewicht weight
Gleitschirm fliegen hang gliding
der Glühwein,-e mulled wine
der Gottesdienst,-e church service
grantig (slang) irritable, unfriendly
griechisch Greek
grob uncouth, coarse
die Größe,-n size
der Großstadttrubel big city stress
die Gründung,-en founding
die Gruppe,-n group
Grüß Gott! "Guten Tag!" (Southern German)
günstig reasonably priced
der Gurt,-e belt
Guten Appetit! Good appetite!
alles Gute! all the best!
das Gymnasium, Gymnasien high school

H

der Hafen,- harbor
die Hälfte,-n one-half
die Halle,-n gym
halt "you know" (slang)
halten von + dat. to think of
der Hamburger,- hamburger
auf die Hand net income after taxes
handeln von to deal with
der Handschuh,-e glove
das Handtuch,¨-er towel
das Handwerk skill, craft
hauptsächlich mainly, for the most part
die Hauptstadt,¨-e capital
die Hauptstraße,-n main street
der Hausberg,-e a name of a mountain
das Haus,¨-er house
  im Haus <u>here:</u> on the job
das Heim,-e home, institution
die Hektik stress, nervousness
hektisch stressful, hectic
der Helm,-e helmet
das Hemd,-en shirt
herrlich splendid
herum/fahren (fährt herum) to move around
die Hexe,-n witch
hin und wieder every now and then
hinaus/treiben (treibt hinaus) to expel, to drive out

im Hintergrund in the background
höchstens at the highest, at the most
die Hochzeit,-en wedding
hoffnungslos hopeless
die Holzmaske,-n wooden mask
der Hopfen hops
der Horrorfilm,-e horror film
die Hose,-n pants
humorvoll witty, humorous

I

das Image image, reputation
immerzu = immer always
Indonesien Indonesia
die Industrie free enterprise
ist so that's how it is

J

die Jacke,-n jacket
das Jackett,-s jacket
das Jahr,-e year
  aus den 60er Jahren from the sixties
je = jemals ever
die Jeans jeans
die Jeansjacke,-n jeans jacket
jedenfalls anyway
jedoch however, yet
der Joghurt,-s yoghurt
die Jugendherberge,-n youth hostel
der Jugendliche,-n teenager, adolescent (masc.)
das Jurastudium education for lawyers

K

das Kabelfernsehen cable TV
der Kaffee coffee
der Kaiserschmarren sweet Austrian pancake
das Kajak,-s kayak
der Kakao cocoa
die Kalorie,-n calorie
die Kameradschaft camaraderie
der Kameramann,¨-er camera operator
kämpfen to fight
die Kampfsportart,-en martial arts
der Kanal,¨-e channel
der Kapitän,-e captain
die Kapuze,-n hood
die Karibik Caribbean
die Kartoffel,-n potato
der Kartoffelsalat,-e potato salad
der Käse,- cheese
die Kaserne,-n barrack
der Kaschmirmantel,¨- cashmere coat
der Kauf,¨-e purchase
  ein guter Kauf a good buy, bargain
der Käufer,- buyer
der Kaufmann,¨-er merchant
kennen/lernen (lernt kennen) to get to know
die Kerze,-n candle
der Kerzenhalter,- candlestick
das Kind,-er child
die Kirche,-n church
kirchlich related to the church
kitschig tacky, kitchy
die Klamotten (coll.) clothes **klassisch** classic
das Kleid,-er dress
die Kleidung clothing
das Kleidungsstück,-e article of clothing
die Kleinigkeit,-en small thing
klettern rock climbing
das Klima climate
knackig crunchy
das Knackwürstchen,- small crunchy sausage
knappe DM 2000 barely 2000 DM
kombinieren to combine
kommen to come
die Konferenz,-en conference
können to be able
  Könnten Sie...? could you?
der Kontakt,-e contact
der Körper,- body
die Körpergröße,-n size
körperlich physical
  die körperliche Fitness physical fitness
das Kostüm,-e costume

die Kraft,¨-e strength, power
die Kreativität,-en creativity
der Krieg,-e war
kriegen = bekommen to get
der Krimi,-s detective story
der Krims-Krams stuff
kritisch critical
der Kuchen,- cake, pie
kucken = gucken (coll.) to watch
hinter die Kulissen schauen to see behind the scenes
die Kultur culture
die Kulturtasche,-n vanity/makeup case
künstlerisch artistic, creative
das Kunstturnen gymnastics
die Kür,-en free skating

L

der Laden,¨- store
die Landschaft,-en landscape, countryside, scenery
langatmig longwinded, boring
langweilig boring
Lanzarote one of the Canary Islands
der Lärm noise
die Lärmbelästigung noise
lässig casual
die Laufbahn,-en career
die Laune,-n mood
die Lebensgewohnheit,-en life style
der Leberkäse,- German meatloaf
lecker delicious
die Lederjacke,-n leather jacket
die Lehre,-n apprenticeship
der Lehrling,-e apprentice
leicht easy
die Leichtathletik track and field
Leipzig big city in Saxony
leisten to afford
die Leistung,-en accomplishment
der Leistungsreiz,-e challenge
der Leistungssportler,- athlete (masc.)
die Leute (pl.) people
die Lieblingssendung,-en favorite program
die Limo,-s = Limonade,-n lemonade, soft drink
die Linie,-n line
  in erster Linie above all, in the first place
der Liter,- liter
locker easy going, relaxed
los loose, free
  es ist (nicht) viel los there is (not) much going on
  los/schicken (schickt los) to send off
die Luft air
  an der frischen Luft in the open air
die Luftverschmutzung air pollution
die Lust (auf) + acc. interest (in)

M

machen to make, do
das macht dick this is fattening
mager lean, skinny
die Mahlzeit,-en meal
der Maibaum,¨-e May pole
zum ersten Mal for the first time
  mal sehen let's see
die Malediven Maldive Islands
manchmal sometimes
männlich masculine
die Mannschaft,-en team
der Mannschaftsgeist = Teamgeist team spirit
manuell manual
die Marmelade,-n jam
der Marsch,¨-e marching
das Material,-ien material
der Mechaniker,- mechanic
die Medizin medicine
die Mehlspeise,-n flour dish
meinen to think
die Meisterprüfung,-en master's exam (vocational)
die Meisterschule,-n school for master students (vocational)
sich melden to report, register
die Menge,-n crowd; <u>here:</u> a lot
die Mensa university dining hall
der Mensch,-en human being; pl. people
die Mentalität,-en character
die Messe,-n trade fair

das Militär military
das Mineralwasser mineral water
das Mitglied,-er member
mit/machen (macht mit) to take part in
mitten in in the middle
mitten im Zentrum right in the center
die Mittlere Reife 10th grade diploma
die Mode,-n fashion
der Modedesigner,- fashion designer
das Model,-s fashion model
moderieren to moderate
die Modewoche,-n week-long fashion exhibit
das Modezentrum,-zentren fashion center
modisch fashionable
die Möglichkeit,-en possibility
momentan these days, at the moment
der Morgenkreis,-e morning circle
motiviert motivated
mürrisch morose
das Museum, pl. **Museen** museum
das Müsli,-s cereal
der Müsliriegel,- cereal bar
die Mütze,-n cap, hat

N

der Nachmittags-Ausblock afternoon duty
die Nachrichten (pl.) news
die Nachrichtensprecherin,-nen anchorwoman
der Nachrichtensprecher,- newscaster, anchorman
nahezu almost
nahrhaft nourishing
das Nahrungsmittel,- food
namhaft well-known, famous
die Natur nature
natürlich naturally; of course, sure
die Naturwissenschaft,-en natural science
nervös nervous
Neuseeland New Zealand
nicht not
  nicht unbedingt not necessarily
nichts nothing
der Normalbürger,- average person
normalerweise normally, usually
nötig necessary
  etwas nötig haben to need something

O

das Obst fruit
öffentlichrechtlich public
das Offizierskasino,-s officer's club
das Olympiastadion,-s Olympic stadium
originell original, unusual
der Ort,-e town

P

das Paar, -e pair, couple
die Palme,-n palm tree
perfekt perfect
die Pfingstferien vacation at Whitsun
pflegerisch nursing
physikalisch physical
der Pilot,-en pilot (masc.)
die Pilotin,-nen pilot (fem.)
die Platte,-n = Schallplatte,-n record
  eine Platte auf/legen (legt auf) to put on a record
plump plump
die Politik politics
die Pommes Frites (pl.) French fries
pompös pompous
das Poster,- poster
das Praktikum pl. **Praktika** practical training
die Praxis here: office
die Presse press
der Profi,-s professional
profihaft as a professional
das Programm,-e channel
der Prospekt,-e brochure
die Prüfung,-en exam, test
  eine Prüfung bestehen to pass an exam
der Pulli,-s sweater
Puma sporting goods company
der Punker,- punk
das Punktspiel,-e playing for points
der Punktspieltag,-e day of competition

Q

der Quark milk product similar to cottage cheese

R

rad/fahren (fährt Rad) to bike
das Radio Xanadu Munich radio station
das Radler,- half beer/half lemonade
der Rapper,- rap (group)
der Ratschlag,¨-e advice
die Raumfahrt space travel
das Recht justice
recht quite
der Rechtsanwalt,¨-e lawyer (masc.)
die Rechtsanwältin,-nen lawyer (fem.)
regelmäßig regularly
reichhaltig rich
reingepreßt crammed into
das Reinigen cleaning
die Reise,-n trip
der Reiz,-e appeal, attraction
reizvoll intriguing
relativ relatively
reparieren to repair
die Restaurantfachfrau,-en restaurant manager
die Riesenauswahl an + dat. enormous choice
der Ring,-e ring
der Rock,¨-e skirt
rodeln to sled
der Rolli,-s turtleneck
der Ruderer,- rower
rudern to row
rum = herum around
der Rundfunk radio
die Rundfunkstation,-en broadcasting station

S

die Sache,-n thing
sagen to say
  würd' ich schon sagen I would say so
das Sakko,-s jacket
der Salat,-e salad
das Salz salt
die Sängerin,-nen singer
schädlich unhealthy, bad
die Schale,-n bowl
scharf spicy, hot
schätzen to guess, presume
schauen (auf) + acc. to look (at)
  es schaut kein Mensch nobody looks you over
das Schaufenster,- display window
der Schauspieler,- actor
die Schauspielerin,-nen actress
die Schauspielschule,-n acting school
der Schellenrührer,- costumed man in carnival pageant
der Schlafanzug,¨-e pajama
schlank slender, thin (people)
schlimm bad
der Schlitten,- sleigh
der Schlittenhund,-e Husky (dog)
der Schlittschuh,-e ice-skating shoe
das Schloß, Schlösser castle
der Schluß end of duty
  zum Schluß finally, in the end
schmecken to taste
  Schmeckt das? Does it taste good?
  Schmeckt's? How does it taste?
der Schnee snow
der Schnitt,-e cut
  im Schnitt on the average
schnitzen to carve
die Schokolade chocolate
schon already
schön beautiful
schreien to scream, cry
der Schriftgenerator,-en titling machine
der Schuh,-e shoe
die Schule,-n school
der Schulabschluß,¨-sse here: education
schulen to train
die Schuluniform,-en uniform
die Schutzausrüstung,-en protective suit
schwer hard
schwerbehindert severely handicapped
schwierig difficult
der See,-n lake

das Segel,- sail
das Segeln sailing
segeln to sail
sehenswert worth seeing
die Sehenswürdigkeit,-en tourist attraction
die Seide silk
seit since, for
die Seite,-n side
selbständig independent; self-employed
selbstbewußt self-confident
das Selbstbewußtsein self-esteem, self-confidence
selbstverständlich sure
der Sender,- station
die Sendung,-en TV program
sensibel sensitive
die Serie,-n series
an sich actually
die Sicherheit,-en certainty, safety
  mit Sicherheit certainly, definitely
sicher sure
  ich bin nicht sicher I'm not sure
siegen = gewinnen to win
die Siegerehrung,-en award ceremony
der Sitzplatz,¨-e seat
der Ski,-er or **Schi** ski
der Skianzug,¨-e ski outfit
ski/fahren (fährt Ski) to ski **ski/laufen (läuft Ski)** to ski
der Skiurlaub ski vacation
das Snowboard,-s snow board
so ein such a
der Socken,- sock
sogar even
das Sojaprodukt,-e soy product
der Soldat,-en soldier
der Sonnenhut,¨-e sun hat
spannen vor to put in front of (a wagon)
die Spannung,-en tension, suspense
der Spaß,¨-e fun
  es macht Spaß it's fun
der Spazierstock,¨-e walking stick
speziell special
das Spiel,-e game
der Spielfilm,-e feature film
die Sportart,-en sports discipline
  eine Sportart treiben to engage in a sport
sportlich athletic
das Sportliche here. athletics
die Sportmedizin sports medicine
der Sportverein sports club
die Sprecherausbildung speech training
das Stadtgründungsfest,-e celebration of city anniversary
der Stadtmensch,-en city person
die Stadtrundfahrt,-en city tour
der Stadtteil,-e part of town, precinct
stärken to strengthen
der Starnberger See lake near Starnberg
statt/finden (findet statt) takes place
stehen to stand
  steht Ihnen (gut)! That suits you (well)!
der Stehplatz,¨-e standing room
die Stelle,-n place, spot
das Stereogerät,-e stereo
der Stiefel,- boot
der Stock,¨-e floor
  im ersten Stock on the second floor
der Stoff,-e material
stolz proud
stören to bother, disturb
der Streit,-e argument, fight
der Streß stress
das Studium, Studien university education
der Stuntman stuntman
super great
das Surfbrett,-er surfboard
das Surfen surfing
surfen to surf
die Süßigkeit,-en sweets, candy
das Sweatshirt,-s sweatshirt
sympathisch pleasant, nice

T

tagespolitische Ereignisse latest political events
der Tänzer,- dancer (masc.)
die Tänzerin,-nen dancer (fem.)
tätig sein to be active, work
die Tätigkeit,-en activity
die Technik technology
technisch technical, mechanical

teil/nehmen (nimmt teil) to participate
der Test,-s test
    einen Test machen to take a test
teuer expensive
der Teufel,- devil
der Therapeut,-en therapist
toll great
der Ton,¨-e sound
der Toningenieur,-e sound engineer
die Torte,-n layer cake, torte
die Touristenzentrale,-n tourist information
die Tracht,-en traditional costume
die Trainerin,-nen female trainer
trainieren to exercise, train
trauen + dat. to trust
treffen (trifft) to meet
das Treiben action
das Trikot,-s sports jersey
der Trubel commotion
tun to do
    ich habe mit ... zu tun I have to deal with...
    zu tun haben mit to deal with
türkisch Turkish
der Turm,¨-e tower
turnen to do gymnastics
typisch typical

U

das U-Boot,-e submarine
die Überbevölkerung overpopulation
das Übergewicht excess weight
    Übergewicht haben to be overweight
überhaupt anyhow
    überhaupt kein not at all
    überhaupt nicht not at all
überladen overburdened, cluttered
sich etwas überlegen to think about something
übernehmen (übernimmt)
    pp. **übernommen** to take over
die Überstunde,-n overtime
überwiegend mostly
übrig left, remaining
    nichts/viel/nicht viel für etwas übrig haben to think nothing/much/not much of something
die Übung,-en exercise
    eine Übung machen to do an exercise
der Umgang interaction
    Umgang haben mit to deal with, to be in touch with
umgebend surrounding
Es geht um ... the topic is ... **die Umwelt** environment
die Umweltverschmutzung pollution
unabhängig independent
ungefähr about, approximately
ungemütlich uncomfortable
ungesund unhealthy
ungewohnt new, unaccustomed
unheimlich eery, uncanny
    unheimlich viel Spaß a lot of fun
unpraktisch impractical, inconvenient
unter der Woche during the week
die Unterhaltung entertainment
unternehmen (unternimmt) to do
sich unterscheiden von to differ from
der Unterschied,-e difference
unzählig countless
der Urlaub vacation

V

der Vegetarier,- vegetarian (masc.)
die Vegetarierin,-nen vegetarian (fem.)
vegetarisch vegetarian
etwas verändern to change something
verbinden to combine
die Verbindung,-en (zwischen + dat.**)** combination (of)
verbringen (mit) to spend (with)
der Verein,-e club, organization, team
verdienen to earn
über etwas verfügen to possess something; to be in charge of something
zur Verfügung stehen to be available
vergleichen mit to compare to
das Vergnügen (sing.) pleasure
    zum Vergnügen for pleasure
der Verkäufer,- salesman
die Verkäuferin,-nen saleswoman

sich verkleiden to dress up
verkleidet dressed up
sich verletzen to hurt oneself
verloren lost
vermeiden to avoid
vermissen to miss
vermitteln here: to give
(das ist) verschieden it varies, it depends
die Verschmutzung pollution
verschönern to beautify
die Verschwendung,-en waste
die Versicherung,-en insurance
der Versicherungsvertreter,- insurance representative
sich verteidigen to defend oneself
der Vertreter,- representative
der Video(film) videotape
vielfältig diverse, interesting
vielseitig multifaceted
der Viktualienmarkt large produce market
der Visagist,-en make-up artist
voll full
  voll mit full of
  am vollsten here: most crowded
das Vollkornprodukt,-e whole grain product
etwas vor/bereiten (bereitet vor) to prepare something
der Vorgang,⸚e here: reaction
sich etwas vor/stellen (stellt sich etwas vor) to imagine something
sich vor/stellen (stellt vor) to introduce oneself
die Voraussetzung,-en precondition

W

die Waffe,-n weapon
die Waffenausbildung,-en arms training
der Wagen,- cart, wagon
wahrscheinlich probably
das Waldsterben dying of the forest
wandern to hike
wär' nichts für mich that's not for me
Das war's. That's it.
das Warenhaus,⸚er department store
die Wasserratte,-n person who is always in the water
die Wasserverschmutzung water pollution
das Wecken waking call
wegen + genitive because of
weg/gehen (geht weg) to go out
weiblich feminine
der Wein,-e wine
weiter further
vieles weiter many other things
das Weizenbier, -e (light) beer
die Welt,-en world
der Weltkrieg,-e world war
die Weltreise,-n trip around the world
die Weltstadt,⸚e metropolis
die Welt world
  aus aller Welt from all over the world
wenn if, when
  wenn's ginge if it were possible
die Werbeagentur,-en marketing company, advertising firm
die Werbung marketing
werden (wird) will (future)
der Wettkampf,⸚e competition, track meet
wichtig important
(Auf) Wiederhören! Bye now! (on the phone)
wider against
widerstehen to withstand temptation
das Wiener Schnitzel veal steak
wieviel, pl. wie viele how much? pl. how many?
der Wintermantel,⸚ winter coat
die Wirtschaft,-en tavern, bar
witzig funny
das Wochenende,-n the weekend
woher? where....from?
die Wohltätigkeit welfare
der Wohltätigkeitszweck,-e welfare purpose
wunderbar wonderful
die Wurst,⸚e sausage
das Würstchen, - small sausage
die Wüste,-n desert

Z

der Zahnarzt,⸚e dentist (masc.)
die Zahnarzthelferin,-nen dental assistant (fem.)
die Zahnärztin,-nen dentist (fem.)

der Zahntechniker,- dental technician
die Zeit,-en time
  nach einer gewissen Zeit after a certain time
  zur Zeit at this time
zeitlos classic
die Zeitverschwendung waste of time
das Zentrum, pl. **Zentren** center
ziehen here: to move, to go
ziemlich rather
die Zigarette,-n cigarette
der Zivi,-s (abbrev. for **Zivildienstleistende,-n**) person doing civilian service
der Zivildienst civilian community service
der Zufall,¨-e contingency, chance
  aus Zufall by chance
zufrieden content
zu/gucken = zu/schauen to watch
der Zuhörer,- listener
der Zuhörerkreis listening audience
die Zukunft future
zunächst first
zu/nehmen (nimmt zu) to gain weight
der Zusammenhalt team spirit
der Zuschauer,- viewer
zu/schicken (schickt zu) to send
der Zweck,-e purpose
der Zweig,-e branch
zwischendurch in between